LOST IN THE STREAM

LOST IN THE STREAM

THE MIRACULOUS STORY OF TWO FISHERMEN LOST AT SEA

CAPT. JOHNNY SAVAGE

THANK YOU FOR TAKING YOUR TIME TO READ THIS STORY WRITTEN BY A FISHERMAN.

Unless otherwise indicated, Bible verses are taken from the following translations:

Holy Bible, New International Version®, NIV® Copyright ©1973, 1978, 1984, 2011 by Biblica, Inc.® Used by permission. All rights reserved worldwide.

Amplified Bible (AMP)

Copyright © 2015 by The Lockman Foundation, La Habra, CA 90631. All rights reserved.

English Standard Version (ESV)

The Holy Bible, English Standard Version. ESV® Text Edition: 2016. Copyright © 2001 by Crossway Bibles, a publishing ministry of Good News Publishers.

King James Version (KJV), Public Domain.

New King James Version (NKJV)

Scripture taken from the New King James Version®. Copyright © 1982 by Thomas Nelson. Used by permission. All rights reserved.

New Living Translation (NLT)

Holy Bible, New Living Translation, copyright © 1996, 2004, 2015 by Tyndale House Foundation. Used by permission of Tyndale House Publishers, Inc., Carol Stream, Illinois 60188. All rights reserved.

New American Standard Bible (NASB)

New American Standard Bible®, Copyright © 1960, 1971, 1977, 1995 by The Lockman Foundation. All rights reserved.

NEW DEGREE PRESS
COPYRIGHT © 2022 CAPT. JOHNNY SAVAGE
All rights reserved.
LOST IN THE STREAM
The Miraculous Story of Two Fishermen Lost at Sea

ISBN		
	979-8-88504-097-6	*Paperback*
	979-8-88504-728-9	*Kindle Ebook*
	979-8-88504-207-9	*Ebook*

This book is primarily dedicated to the Lord my God. Thank you for forgiveness through the blood and saving two lost fishermen.

I dedicate this book to my wife and children. I love each one of you so very much. Samantha, you are the love of my life, and I never could have accomplished this without your support.

I dedicate this book to anyone who has ever felt lost, overwhelmed, and alone. Never lose hope and never give up.

Cover Photo: I would like to thank Captain VJ Bell for providing the photo of the charter boat, UNBELIEVABLE. StuartBigGame.com Kevin Francis operating drone.

CONTENTS

DEAR READER — 11

PART 1.   **TOSSED AT SEA** — 17

CHAPTER 1.   *ANHINGA* UNDERWAY — 19
CHAPTER 2.   MAYDAY DENIED — 33
CHAPTER 3.   ABANDON SHIP IS NO SEA SPORT — 41
CHAPTER 4.   HIGH HOPES FOR THE EPIRB — 51
CHAPTER 5.   JUST ONE MORE PICTURE — 65
CHAPTER 6.   IMPULSIVE HOPE — 71
CHAPTER 7.   A SPECK ON THE HORIZON — 83
CHAPTER 8.   ROUGH SEAS AND FADING HOPE — 93
CHAPTER 9.   RELEASE ME FROM THE CHAOS — 107
CHAPTER 10.   DIVINE INTERVENTION — 115
CHAPTER 11.   *DESPERADO* TO BE SAVED — 127
CHAPTER 12.   SAVED BY GRACE! — 139
CHAPTER 13.   A FATHER'S LOVE — 149
CHAPTER 14.   RETURNING HOME — 159
CHAPTER 15.   THE DEPOSITION — 171
CHAPTER 16.   FIRST TIME BACK OUT ON THE MONSTER — 179

PART 2.	THE ANATOMY OF A MIRACLE	**187**
CHAPTER 17.	THE SCIENCE	189
CHAPTER 18.	MAJOR MOTION ON THE SEA	197
CHAPTER 19.	CONTANGO AND EPISODES OF A CAPTAIN	207

PART 3.	TELLING THE STORY AND CHANGING LIVES	**215**
CHAPTER 20.	POLICE, SEALS, AND A SNIPER—LIFE IS PRECIOUS	217
CHAPTER 21.	NO PROBLEM CRYING OUT	225
CHAPTER 22.	TOUCHING OTHERS	233
CHAPTER 23.	IN THE ADMIRAL'S HANDS	245
CHAPTER 24.	CROSSING THROUGH DANGEROUS WATERS	253

PART 4.	APPENDIX OF STORIES—ADVENTURES OF THE GOON	**259**
FISH STORY 1.	MONKEY BUSINESS	261
FISH STORY 2.	THE PRINCESS, THE GOLDFISH, AND THE BLEEDING MACKEREL	265

ACKNOWLEDGMENTS	273
GLOSSARY	279
APPENDIX	285

The Armor of God

10 Finally, be strong in the Lord and in his mighty power. 11 Put on the full armor of God, so that you can take your stand against the devil's schemes. 12 For our struggle is not against flesh and blood, but against the rulers, against the authorities, against the powers of this dark world and against the spiritual forces of evil in the heavenly realms. 13 Therefore put on the full armor of God, so that when the day of evil comes, you may be able to stand your ground, and after you have done everything, to stand. 14 Stand firm then, with the belt of truth buckled around your waist, with the breastplate of righteousness in place, 15 and with your feet fitted with the readiness that comes from the gospel of peace. 16 In addition to all this, take up the shield of faith, with which you can extinguish all the flaming arrows of the evil one. 17 Take the helmet of salvation and the sword of the Spirit, which is the word of God.

—EPHESIANS 6: 10-17 NIV

The miracle of the story.
You were in God's current, not of the world's current. In the end, He intended you to be saved in His current. Showed you miracles in His current. The world's current went by, showing no help of saving you. Like life, He knows, we're in His current, intended to be saved. But like He said, we have to pick our line and paddle it. He won't make the choices for us. We were made in his image in the world but not of it. He wants to save us in the end. We can choose to go with the current of the world or we can see His miracles and paddle to His safety. Being tossed around in this world can make survival seem impossible, stuck in an ebb, highs and lows of one white cap to the next, terrified of the unknowns beneath and around you. Cry out for God. He'll show you the current to get in. He'll save you in the end.

—SAMANTHA SAVAGE

DEAR READER,

I'm writing you this letter while sitting at a lakeside park bench across the street from the SEAL Heritage Center on a Naval Base in Virginia Beach, Virginia. I'm humbled by the thought of all the sacrifices made by these warriors and their families. Who am I, that these brave American heroes have asked me to share the story of the fishing vessel *Anhinga* with them? I was intrigued by why members of this elite group would care about my story. They lovingly, willingly, and fearlessly put their lives at risk for others as a service to these great United States of America. How could my story possibly benefit them? I did not understand. So, I asked. The answer was simple: *hope*. This story gives them hope that the God they pray to is real; hope that if the next mission results in a sacrifice of the last full measure, they will see heaven; and hope in the prayer emblazoned on the wall for any visitor who enters the building behind me to view:

> *Dear Father in Heaven, if I may respectfully say so, sometimes you are a strange God. Though you love all mankind, it seems you have special predilections too. You seem to love those men who can stand alone, who face impossible odds, who challenge every bully*

and every tyrant—those men who know the heat and loneliness of a Calvary. Possibly You cherish men of this stamp because You recognize the marks of your only Son in them. Since this unique group of men known as the SEALs know Calvary and suffering, teach them now the mystery of the resurrection—that they are indestructible, that they will live forever because of their deep faith in You. And when they do come to Heaven, may I respectfully warn You, dear Father, they also know how to celebrate. So please be ready for them when they insert under your pearly gates.

Bless them, their devoted families, and their country on this glorious occasion. We ask this through the merits of your Son, Christ Jesus the Lord, Amen.

—BY CHAPLAIN E.J. MCMALHON
LIEUTENANT COMMANDER
PRESIDENTIAL UNIT CITATION
CEREMONY IN 1975 FOR SEAL TEAM 1

Every now and then, a story comes along so powerful it touches and changes lives. This is one of those stories. Twenty-three years ago today, the names of Eric Bingham (captain) and I, Johnny Savage (mate), should have been logged in the book of fishermen to go to sea and never return. On April 13, 1998, the sportfishing vessel *Anhinga* was struck by a rogue wave ninety nautical miles out to sea. The periling encounter occurred in the Gulf Stream current as the *Anhinga* was in transit from Key West, Florida, to Cancún, Mexico. This is the story of two fishermen whose lives would be forever changed by the crisis.

This is the story of a fight for survival with every ounce of strength in an environment the human body was not created to withstand. There were moments of great hope followed by crushing blows of loss. The sea conditions were beautiful, and they were horrific. We were out there alone, and no one knew the *Anhinga* was lost forever. Being alone is one of a human's greatest fears from the moment they exist in the womb.

Rarely did either of us tell the story ourselves. Many secondhand accounts of the event were told by others in all kinds of settings. The events of that fateful day changed the way vessels make open ocean transits in the sportfishing industry. Occasionally, Eric or I share the story of the *Anhinga* with a friend if conditions are just right.

Everyone reaches low points in their lives. What brings you out of those dark places? For me, it's faith and gratitude. I pray this story will give hope to the lost, faith to the faithless, encouragement to those facing overwhelming odds against them, and provide proof that miracles do happen.

Years after the *Anhinga* went down, I was a safety engineer for Ford Motor Company. A coworker asked me, "Johnny, why do you always have a smile on your face? Why are you always so happy?" I replied, "Every day on this Earth is a gift from God, and I am truly grateful to be alive today."

What happened to cause me to finally open up and share all of the details about the fight for survival that Captain Eric and I went through? In short, I was in a very dark place in my life, and the Holy Spirit moved in my heart. *It's time to tell the story.* I didn't want to because only writers write books, and I'm just a fisherman. I resisted, then relented and obeyed. I've been sharing the story with various groups ever since. Many have said, "You have to write a book about this." In my opinion, the last section of the book is the most powerful. I will bring you into my greatest fear. We will also go inside the sportfishing industry and some of the science related to what happened out there. But first, you must witness the power of the story of the *Anhinga*.

Please open your heart to allow this story to reach into the depths of your soul and give you hope in whatever situation you have been through, are going through, or will be on your horizon. Allow this story to give, grow, and restore faith.

With faith, hope, and love,
Captain Johnny

Captain Johnny at the helm of the *Just One More*.

The fifty-six-foot sportfishing vessel, *Anhinga* (of Port Aransas, Texas), a beautiful custom-built Jim Smith Tournament Boat.

PART 1:

TOSSED AT SEA

CHAPTER 1:

ANHINGA UNDERWAY

The spring of 1998 was approaching, and Captain Gary knew the sportfishing boat *Major Motion* had just been listed by the owners. "Little" Jimmy, the captain of the *Major Motion*, told me he would understand if I looked for a mate's job on another boat. He knew well of the uncertainty of working on a boat that was for sale. Plus, the charter fishing season at Sailfish Marina in Palm Beach, Florida, would be slowing down. Captain Gary, a friend of mine from Virginia Beach, knew I wanted to get back on a private boat for the upcoming Mexico sailfish season.

Gary arranged for me to meet Captain Eric Bingham who ran a beautiful, custom-built, fifty-six-foot Jim Smith called the *Anhinga*. I had never worked on a Jim Smith boat before, but I had always wanted to.

A meeting had been arranged for Eric and I to meet on the boat at Sailfish Marina in Stuart, Florida. In the sportfishing world, there are generally no job applications and few résumés. Reputations are everything. Gary's word was good enough for Captain Eric and I to start planning to fish the Chub Cay Marlin Tournament. My first impression of the captain was, *He has a cool Australian accent.*

I grew up in the rural southeastern corner of Virginia Beach, Virginia, where playmates were few and a fishing pole was one of my best friends. Mother used to scream for me to come home for supper and my father would say to her, "You're wasting your time. That boy is fishing, he won't be home until the fish quit biting."

Blackwater is the name of the small borough I grew up in. The name of the area was fitting due to the cypress swamps that stain the water to look like straight black coffee. The swamps were filled with water moccasin snakes, or cotton mouths as we call them due to the pure white color inside their mouth that appears as a bright white flash when they strike.

This was a very close-knit community where neighbors looked out for each other and all was centered through the local church, which was founded in 1774. Although I had taken it for granted, the little Blackwater Baptist Church with a big heart played a major role in my life.

I first started making money fishing by helping my dad gill net when I was twelve. When I turned sixteen, I started working as a mate for Captain Fred Feller on the head boats out of Rudee Inlet. While in college, I switched from dealing with the masses of tangled-lines tourist on head boats to the glory of offshore charter boats, which carried up to six passengers fishing for Gulf Stream pelagic species of fish.

The thrill of catching tuna, mahi, and marlin was much better than the constant congestion of tangled fishing lines. I was twenty-five years old going on my ninth year as a mate in 1997. I left Virginia the day after Christmas for my second season working in Florida. The charter season in the Palm Beach area was centered around the winter sailfish migration from the end of December through the beginning of March.

Following the migration patterns of the fish is how professional sportfishermen pay the bills.

Prior to becoming a captain, Eric had several other careers helping to build his peaceful and patient character. One of the jobs was inspired by a friend who had an idea to make some fast Aussie cash from what nature had provided. It was simply a matter of getting a gun, a boat, a little courage, and some go-get-it.

Eric showed up for his first day on the new job, which was when he found out they were going hunting for crocodiles. The cash would come from selling their hides. They loaded up on the boat and were on their way to the croc grounds. Eric's friend had little knowledge about the venture.

Eric's friend enlightened him on how the process would go down. They would ease up on the croc, and his friend would shoot the croc in the head. Because crocs sink, Eric would have to quickly jump in just as he shot and grab the toothy monster. Naturally, Eric asked the question, "What happens if you miss?"

In 1967, Captain Eric was traveling around the world and decided he wanted to see the America's Cup Sailboat Race. He was in British Columbia, Canada, when he met another fella who wanted to see the races. The two adventurers jumped into a 1958 Chevy Station Wagon and drove all the way across North America to Newport, Rhode Island. Once Eric arrived in Rhode Island, he met up with some buddies he used to sail with back home in Sydney.

After the Cup races, Eric didn't really have a plan. That's when he made some new friends who asked him, "Where are you going to go next?"

"I was thinking about maybe going to South America to see what was going on down there," Eric replied.

"Well, if you're going through Florida, we got the name of some people you could look up if you want. Seeing as how you were in boating in Australia," his new friends said.

Eric was then Florida bound. Once he arrived, he started meeting people, and one thing led to another. Eric ended up working on fishing boats out of Bahia Mar in Fort Lauderdale. He had crossed the line. Eric had gone from the dark side to the light side. Or, from a sail boater's perspective, he was a traitor for defecting. There has always been a sort of tension between the high-speed sportfishing world and the laid-back slow-paced sailboat world.

I was extremely excited about getting started the next week on one of the fastest boats in the industry. I was also excited about working with a captain who would be able to teach me the art of working Dacron. Dacron is a type of fishing line made of woven polyester fibers. Captain Eric and I would take the *Anhinga* from Stuart, Florida, across the Gulf Stream to the Bahamas. We would be fishing a blue marlin tournament in Chub Cay. Our week-long fishing adventure was going to be sort of a test of personalities prior to making the three-month journey to Cancún, Belize, and Guatemala. I think I was most excited about the family atmosphere. I always loved to see an owner and their family enjoy a boat together. It had been a few months since I had seen my own family.

The job was one of the best paying private boat jobs around, and I really wanted to do a good job. Most of my prior fishing career was on charter boats. The *Anhinga* was a private boat with an owner from Port Aransas, Texas. Everything depended on how I was able to get along with the owner and his family. Private boat jobs require more catering to the wants and needs of the owner and their guests, whereas in charter fishing, the main goal is to make sure the party catches fish and has fun. Charter customers couldn't care less about which direction the labels on the drinks or canned vegetables are facing. When it comes down to it, the owners of the private sportfishing yachts own them because they want to catch fish and have fun.

Captain Eric and I crossed over and set up in our slip at the Chub Cay Club, in the Berry Islands of the Bahamas. The next morning, we had an hour run to cross the thirty nautical miles to Lyford Cay, a private resort on the west end of Nassau Island. Lyford is where we got tied up waiting for the owner, his wife, and his daughter to arrive. My focus was on doing what I knew best: preparing the fishing tackle for the tournament. I had not asked many questions about the family I would be spending three months with on a fifty-six-foot boat.

I was so nervous about meeting the new boss and family. I only knew a few things about them. The owner had a custom Merritt's sportfish boat prior to buying the Jim Smith boat. His friends called him "Jay-Bird," which is why he named his boat after a fishing bird. He and his wife were super-nice, fun-loving people who enjoyed traveling on their boat—fishing, diving, and exploring. The only thing I knew about the daughter was that we were about the same age and this was going to be a well-deserved trip for her to relax.

I was down below organizing some stuff in the front of the boat when I could hear Eric outside in the cockpit talking to someone. I looked and saw bags being passed down. *Oh, no! The mate on private boats always needs to be in the cockpit to greet owners and assist the ladies aboard. I failed big time.* The salon door was opened where I could easily see the boss and his wife step on. My heart raced with nervousness as I scrambled to close the storage hatch I was working in. I got it closed and turned to rush up to the deck to introduce myself. Then my nerves were an absolute wreck as I saw the boss's daughter step on. She was beautiful. Captain Eric should have given me a heads-up on that one.

Introductions were made and bags were stored away. Then we ran back to Chub for our week of tournament festivities. The week was amazing. We were all together almost the entire time. During the day, we were all on the *Anhinga* fishing. At night, we had dinner as a fishing team. In the evening, after cleaning the boat, it was the only time I was away. For some strange reason, I had an urge from within my soul to push the limits of my ability to swim.

Everyone on board the *Anhinga* appeared to have a great time together. At least, I did. It was a dream job until I had to go back to charter fishing. Captain Eric and the boss's family were great to work for. The boss and his wife were fun-loving people whose actions painted a portrait of love for each other. The boss's daughter was a real joy to hang out with, and she didn't shy away from a day of fishing on choppy seas.

The trip went very well except for when Eric and I were running back across the Gulf Stream returning to the *Anhinga*'s home port in Stuart. There was a little bit of a side-to swell on the way home, which caused the *Anhinga* to rock from side to side occasionally. It was time for a mid-trip inspection of the interior of the boat to see how everything was riding. When I opened the salon doors, it looked like a bomb had gone off in the galley.

The refrigerator was located on the port outboard side of the galley along with the freezer. With one of the waves, the refrigerator door swung open into the aisle leading to the hallway. When the door opened, everything from the mayonnaise to the pickles fell out onto the floor. The floor was like a Slip 'N Slide. This was a good lesson learned prior to making the long run to Mexico. I now knew another great mayonnaise escape must be prevented.

April 11 was the day of departure for the run from Stuart down to Key West to stage for our weather window to make the three-hundred-fifty-mile crossing to Mexico. When I woke up, I had a serious dilemma to deal with that morning because of something I had not talked to Eric about. Cancún could have pretty good waves at times, and a surfboard usually went everywhere I did.

Aunt Donna and Uncle Joe made arrangements to take me and my surfboard to the boat on the morning of our departure from Stuart. I figured the worst thing Eric could say was to leave it behind. When he let me bring it along, I was really excited about working for him. The only requirement was that it would have to ride in my bunk up in the very front of the boat. After big goodbye hugs, Captain Eric climbed up to the helm, and I cast off the lines. Aunt Donna took pictures with a freebie, disposable *Sports Illustrated* camera she'd found somewhere.

That afternoon, the *Anhinga* arrived at Oceanside Marina in Key West. Eric and I rinsed the salt off her and went out for a well-deserved dinner. The next day was all about washing the *Anhinga* first thing in the morning. The rest of the day was spent polishing her up. The thirteen-plus hours of run to Cancún was hard on an unprotected exterior finish. The polish would make it easier to clean off the black diesel soot that would cover the beautiful, baby-blue yacht with her tuna tower that reached toward the sky.

Our plan on the morning of April 13, 1998, was to get underway at five o'clock in the morning to make sure we would arrive at our destination before nightfall. The first priority, however, was Captain Eric's Breakfast Special. I enjoyed my last American freshwater shower while Eric prepared the toasted bagels with a smoked salmon spread. They were topped with a perfectly sliced fresh tomato and sprinkled with a light dusting of fresh-ground black pepper. They were absolutely delicious.

After the second round, Eric put the perishables back into the refrigerator.

This refrigerator and I did not get along very well. My favorite napping spot on the *Anhinga* was on the floor in the aisle just above the steps leading down to the forward berthing area of the boat, with my back against the untrustworthy door of my nemesis.

Captains and mates perform a standard mental checklist every time a boat leaves the slip. Several more items are added to the list if the boat is not returning to that particular port, and yet more items are added when making an open-sea crossing out of the country. Our passports, boat documents, and yellow quarantine flag were in order and ready to clear the Mexican customs agency. The oil, fuel, electronics, and weather had been checked. I removed the nonessential mooring lines. The generator and motors were running smoothly. I stored the water hoses and shore power cable. One of the many boat etiquette rules includes: You never stink up the inside of the boat by taking a dump in the head when you can go somewhere else. Therefore, the "kids had been dropped off in the pool" by the marina ship's store.

One item remained to be resolved prior to pulling out of the slip. What were we going to do with the emergency position indicating radio beacon (EPIRB) and life raft? The marine life safety devices had been sitting in the middle of the salon floor for three days, so we had been stepping over and around them.

We wondered whether we should put the EPIRB and life raft outside on the deck of the cockpit for the run.

These items were often kept out of the weather and soot. Otherwise, they would have to be cleaned upon arriving to our destination.

We would be getting to Mexico late in the evening, and we already had enough to clean up. Besides, "nothing ever happens during the daytime."

Facing the back of the boat, I looked toward the right. The sun was rising off our port stern quarter as we left the Northwest Channel behind us. Captain Eric pushed forward on the throttle levers. I could hear the revolutions begin to increase on the pair of German-made MAN diesel engines. The air began to whistle as it passed through the two turbos on each of the 820-horsepower engines. The forced air and increased fuel in the massive diesel engines gave the *Anhinga* a boost of power. My feet could sense the rapid vibration as the *Anhinga*'s bottom rose up out of the water at her low-cruising speed.

I thought about how that evening my senses would return to the environment they had left behind ten months ago—the *Yucatan*. The simple things of God's creation always brought me peace when I was far from my Virginia home. After long crossings at sea, the songs of birds, chirps of insects, and smells of vegetation were always so unique to each port we were entering.

The sea conditions were beautiful as I sat on the flybridge with Captain Eric at the helm—a light easterly breeze with a following sea of two to three feet. I wished Captain Milton and Neil—his teenage son—were with us for this crossing. It was always nice to have extra hands aboard. Milton and

I agreed, however, that the El Niño weather patterns made our planned transit too unpredictable. Milton could easily book flights only to end up stuck in Key West if the weather didn't allow us a window to make the trip across the lower Gulf of Mexico.

The operating position on most sportfishing boats is located at an exterior elevated position known as the flybridge. The captain and guests on the bridge are typically protected from the elements by clear plastic curtains. These curtains fully enclose the area across the front of the flybridge and down both sides to protect the helm area from salty sea spray, wind storms, and rain storms. The flybridge of the *Anhinga* did not have a full front enclosure. A single curtain located in front of the bridge console blocked the wind and sea spray. The helm was at the vessel's centerline, and the rest of the console extended to the port side of the bridge. The *Anhinga*'s VHF communication radios and some of the other essential marine electronics were in the port side section of the console. The helm chair was the only seating behind the protection of the curtain.

We were in the open water to the South-Southwest of Key West. I stood, leaning against the port side of the bridge and listening to Eric tell stories of his adventures in sportfishing as he set our final course heading just off the Northern tip of Isla Mujeres. This "Island of Women" is five miles long by half a mile wide and is located just off Cancún, Mexico. Isla Mujeres is pretty calm, or "tranquillo" as the natives would say. Personally, the place had always creeped me out. How many virgins had the ancient Mayans sacrificed on this small island?

As entertaining as Captain Eric's stories were, we had a lot of water to put behind us, and I was getting tired of standing.

No tasks needed to be completed, so I decided it was time to take a nap. I had been up late the previous night chasing the protected tarpon in the basin of Oceanside Marina. I was fishing after the marina staff went home for the night.

For some reason, I decided to take a nap on the flybridge, front bench. Maybe I was trusting the refrigerator, maybe I wanted to be on standby for Eric, or maybe I was missing home and all the days of charter fishing on the *High Hopes* out of Virginia Beach. Captain Dave and I took turns napping on the flybridge's bench seat during our two-hour runs to and from the fishing grounds. Regardless of the reason, it was going to be chilly in front of the single curtain, and my foul weather gear was in the cabin below.

Captain Eric noticed where I was headed and called out, "Hey, buddy, do a quick walk-through while you're down there to make sure everything is good."

"No problem," I replied.

Everything looked secure. The stateroom, head, and shower doors were locked into position, nothing was loose on the counter or floor to slide around, and thankfully the refrigerator door was behaving. With board shorts and a Chub Cay Club T-shirt on, I stepped into one of those thick orange Grundens Herkules bibs, then climbed up to the bridge with the matching jacket. Eric received the follow-up report that everything was holding secure below. With the rain slickers breaking the wind in front of the flybridge console, I stretched out on the thin, well broken-in foam cushion for a peaceful nap. The problem was, I couldn't sleep because I was so excited about getting to Mexico—all the sailfish we would catch and hanging out with the boat owner's family. I tossed and turned for what seemed like forever. Suddenly, a loud *bang* that came from below sounded like two pieces of timber smashing into each other. The sound startled both of us, but we could tell the sound was not structural. I jumped up. I expected to see that something had gotten loose or something slid from the bait-station, and fell onto the teak wood deck of the cockpit. Eric gave the orders to go down and investigate as he slowed the *Anhinga* to idle speed. Turned out, it was the double doors that led into the salon of the boat.

The starboard side salon was freely rolling on the overhead track, and as the boat rolled, it would slide open and then roll back and strike the port side door. The clamp had come loose on the cable that held the door in a fixed position. I reported the situation up to the bridge and asked the captain to pull the throttles back to idle. The *Anhinga* had a beautiful interior. I was afraid if I tried to retighten the clamp while underway, I might damage the wood trim if I slipped.

With the door fixed, I went back up on the bridge to inform Eric of the details of the repair. Standing to his starboard side, where the open aisle leads around to the front of the bridge, Eric and I looked at each other as he started to slowly ease the throttles up.

I said, "She's holding good, but that screw needs some Loctite put on it tonight."

Just as I said this, we both looked forward into what had been a fairly calm sea to see the unimaginable. It was like a hole had opened up into the ocean. It was every mariner's nightmare—a rogue wave, and the fifty-six-foot *Anhinga* was about to free-fall down the face of it like the first drop of a roller-coaster ride.

Captain Eric (foreground) and Mate Johnny (me) are preparing the *Anhinga* to depart from Sailfish Marina in Stuart, Florida. On April 11, 1998, the *Anhinga* went down the coast to stage at Oceanside Marina in Key West, Florida, where we waited for a window of good weather to cross the Gulf of Mexico to Cancún.

CHAPTER 2:

MAYDAY DENIED

Once the *Anhinga*'s bow had extended into the hole beyond her center of gravity, everything changed. It felt like I was free-falling forward past the starboard side of the console until slamming into the front cap of the flybridge enclosure. I grabbed a hold of a small rail attached to the cap and the front starboard tower leg. There was not a front curtain to prevent a future free fall out the front of the bridge and down onto the bow deck, so I began to duck below that front cap as her bow struck the bottom of the wave. What happened in an instant felt like an eternity of plummeting.

I wondered, *How could this be? How could I be free-falling forward when her bow hasn't even stuffed into the next wave? How is it possible for such a massive wave, hole, or whatever this is to exist? How could a single wave be so different? The wave was so much larger than the two- to three-foot waves we were running with. It must have been one of those rogue waves.*

The force of gravity had pulled her bow down and caused her to accelerate at a nearly vertical angle until she plunged into the trough with a loud breaking sound as she hit the bottom of the wave. The *Anhinga* crashed into the bottom of the wave with such force that my already falling body slammed into the forward part of the flybridge with a thud. When the point of the *Anhinga*'s bow penetrated the water, the pressure of the seawater pushing in on the front and sides of the hull must have been enormous. I remember being struck by water, but I do not know where it came from. My ears were filled with a loud and horrific sound that's terrifying to mariners. The sound of her structural bulkheads breaking. That's when I saw the dooming crack in the bow deck. It was about a foot in front of where the house of the cabin meets the bow deck. It began on her outboard starboard and ran across toward the port side.

The *Anhinga* was broken in one of the most structurally critical areas. Seeing the separation of the bow deck was so surreal. My entire being was gripped with fear due to the impending circumstance. My heart and soul felt like they were being squeezed with a crushing force. The *Anhinga* was falling apart. She was our security and the stable foundation below our feet. She was the separation between us and the unforgiving sea. In an instant, Captain Eric and I had gone from joy and confidence to an all-encompassing fear. I knew it was going to be hard on my parents to lose their only son.

In years of professional sportfishing, I had never seen anything close to this rogue, powerful force of nature. Behind the protection of the helm, Eric was able to quickly pull her transmissions out of gear as her bow fell forward. If the captain had not been able to bring the *Anhinga*'s motors to idle and the gears to neutral position, the vessel would have propelled herself into the bottom of the hole with a much greater force, causing much greater damage to her and serious injury to Eric and me. In Eric's many salty decades, he had never seen such a force either. Many people have asked, "How big was the wave?" I cannot say for certain because I was falling forward as the *Anhinga* rushed down the face of it. I do know the *Anhinga* was fifty-six feet in length with a flybridge position more toward the aft, or rear as is the case with all sportfishing vessels. Everything within my peripheral vision was in the wave.

The sight of the rogue wave was the scariest thing I had ever seen in my life. My terror was rooted in the realization of the massive beast's sheer power. It had been roaming the sea surface looking for a vessel to devour. The wave was much like Satan was reported to have roamed the earth in the book of Job.

Our speed at the time we fell off the wave was so slow that our current situation seemed impossible. I remember wondering, *How could so much destruction have occurred without the boat even being at a low cruising speed?* It was so effortless for the wave to totally destroy something in seconds that had taken the many craftsmen at Jim Smith Tournament Boats approximately a year to build.

I still expected to feel the mighty bow of the *Anhinga* rise even though my eyes saw her bow deck break loose and my ears heard her bulkheads breaking. The thought was short-lived as reality crashed before me. Soaked from being struck by seawater, I turned to Eric and shouted, "Oh my God! She is going down!" He didn't have the same vantage point to see the utter destruction of the bow-deck. He quickly turned to his left and began to reach down to initiate a marine distress sequence. Eric was reaching for the very high frequency (VHF) marine communication radio to broadcast the most feared words of any mariner: "Mayday! Mayday! Mayday! This is the fishing vessel, *Anhinga, Anhinga, Anhinga.*" The only thing more terrifying is what happened next. While Captain Eric was in mid-reach for the radio microphone, he stopped reaching. The VHF radio is one of the most important safety devices on any vessel, and its power source had already been destroyed by the sea. For us, there would not be a mayday transmission broadcast to the US Coast Guard or any other vessel for that matter.

I've been present to assist other vessels in distress that were taking on water and going down. One of those incidents occurred offshore of Ocean City, Maryland, where a sportfish boat had struck a submerged object while running to the Continental Shelf during the White Marlin Open Fishing Tournament. The submerged object had created a hole in its bottom that was allowing more water to come into the hull than the bilge pumps could remove. As the vessel settled below the water with only the flybridge exposed, the radar antenna on top of the flybridge continued to make its revolutions. The batteries that powered the electronics must have been in an air pocket since they were about ten feet below the water.

Time in relation to water intrusion is a critical factor in marine emergencies. The boat off Ocean City had about an hour with a moderate rate of flooding until settling, yet it never sank. For Eric and I, it was almost an instantaneous complete flooding of the *Anhinga*'s hull. The impact force of the rogue wave the *Anhinga* encountered was so violent that the seawater crushingly penetrated the hull and spread throughout the engine room. Her batteries in the engine room were shorted out; therefore, the VHF radios had no power to transmit a distress call.

Without a distress call, our only hope for notifying the Coast Guard was with the emergency position indicating radio beacon (EPIRB). Captain Eric then gave his command, "Get the life jackets, buddy." He turned and dropped down the ladder into the cockpit with the same speed and determination as a firefighter sliding down the pole to save lives in a roaring structural fire.

I darted from my position on the front right corner to the front left corner of the flybridge. The life jackets were stored in a locker located inside the flybridge seating area, which was forward of the helm console. I tossed aside the thin four-foot seat cushion to gain access to the port side hatch cover. I used the finger hole to remove the baby blue plywood hatch and noticed another potentially fatal marine safety error.

Anyone who has ever taken a road trip with their family knows storage space is valuable, and the longer the trip the more precious the storage is. We were planning on being out of the country for a few months. It's amazing the *Anhinga* could even get out of her slip in Stuart, Florida, with all the extra gear. The dock freezer, food, bait, rum, poly-ball fenders, coolers, and tent used to escape the Yucatan sun all must have a place to be securely stored. The filmmakers of *The Perfect Storm* did an outstanding job in the scene where the crew is loading a truck load of supplies on Andrea Gail in preparation for an extended trip.

The *Anhinga* was rapidly going down. I tried desperately to follow the instruction given to get the life jackets. There was stuff packed away and stored on top of the floatation devices in the tight compartment. Although I was able to easily remove the smaller items, somehow, we had managed to fit the pop-up tent in the hatch. Lying across the life jackets, it was trapping them down underneath. I quickly glanced forward to see how fast the *Anhinga* was sinking. This was my first time taking a glance forward since announcing she was going down. It was happening quick. The *Anhinga* was going down bow first at a sharp angle and listing to the port side. Time was of the essence. Grabbing the tent's storage bag, I shuffled and pulled with every ounce of strength I had, but it would not move enough to free the life jackets. With the flybridge about to go under, I had no choice but to abort mission. I struggled with the knowledge this failure could cost us our lives.

The thought of what I was about to do was surreal. Abandoning ship is always the last resort. If I didn't move quickly, I would be trapped on the flybridge and pulled under with the boat. I escaped being entrapped on the flybridge by stepping off the forward bridge cap on the portside cap and directly into the water. It was only about eighteen inches from the cap to the waterline. All hope was now in Eric's ability to successfully get in the cabin to extract the EPIRB and life raft. The life raft had been certified and packed into a valise case similar to a duffle bag. I swam toward the stern along what little bit of the *Anhinga*'s left side remained above water. I reached the open deck of the cockpit and, to my horror, discovered Captain Eric beating on the salon doors in an attempt to get inside the cabin.

Just inside the cabin was the safety gear that was our final chance at life. He was punching the small glass panels as hard as he could. If Eric could break the glass, he might be able to reach in and grab the EPIRB. There was no need to try to open the doors. They were wedged in their closed position by the twisting of the boat's hull and structure. The small panels of glass were just too strong for Eric to break. Captain Eric was within a few feet of the most vital of all marine safety equipment, but the jammed doors were not going to allow him access.

This all happened in less than a couple of minutes. As I treaded water over the port covering board, I felt something pulling me downward. It was the rope of the halyard line from the outrigger. The line was pulling across my shoulder as the boat sank. I looked up to see the riggers, antennas, tuna tower, and other gear, and fear overcame me. There was so much above us that we could be caught on or between. She was going to take us down with her.

Photo of the Anhinga as I removed the unnecessary dock lines from the starboard side of the boat prior to departing Stuart, Florida.

CHAPTER 3:

ABANDON SHIP IS NO SEA SPORT

When I looked up there was sight of the tuna tower reaching toward the sky. The tower is a structure designed to give the crew the advantage of height to see further across the horizon and down deeper into that beautiful blue water. A tuna tower somewhat resembles the structure of a high voltage power line tower. There were four legs mounted to the deck with two ladder sections on each of the aft outer legs to access the upper control station. "X" bracing links between each of the tower legs help to give the massive structure support as the sportfish navigates the forces exerted by rough seas. Four, sixteen-foot, white fiberglass, marine antennas extended above the upper control station to give the best possible range for the VHF radios.

There was one outrigger on each side of the boat used to stretch our baits out into a wide pattern as they are pulled behind the boat on the surface of the water. The riggers on the *Anhinga* were forty-feet long with triple-spreader bars. The spreader bars use an "X" bracing system to support tension cables that hold the weight of the long metal poles.

Halyard lines form a scalene triangle by running through connection points on the outrigger and then pass through a pulley positioned on the gunwale for each side of the cockpit. Adjustable release clips are fastened to the main halyard line. The halyards act similar to the haul line on a flagpole. The halyard line is typically run with the monofilament line having a four- to six-hundred-pound breaking strength.

The *Anhinga*'s port outrigger looming above my head presented a number of opportunities to take us down with her. If I had become tangled in the halyard line, I would have never been able to break free by my own strength. It was almost as if the line going across my shoulder was a tap on the shoulder from God saying, "I am with you, but you are in danger. Look up."

I didn't think the *Anhinga* was going under with enough mass and speed to cause a suction effect. I calculated the downward suction effect wouldn't be greater than our ability to escape it. However, it certainly did not change the intensity of the fear, especially not when I surveyed the rest of my surroundings. From my position of treading water on the port side of the cockpit, I could see there were so many possibilities for Captain Eric or me to become entangled or trapped. We would have to pass through segments of the tuna tower and rigging as she went down. We would be like a child weaving our way through a jungle gym of jagged obstacles. We were most certainly in grave danger.

Eric was still relentlessly attempting to free the jammed doors. In that moment, I shouted to Eric, who was unable to see the doom hovering over us, "We have to get away from this thing before it takes us down with it!" The first of a series of amazing miracles was about to occur. The *Anhinga* was going down too fast for there to be any hope of getting the EPIRB or life raft. It was time to abandon ship again. For some reason, Eric and I had both cleared toward her rear and off the stern. The exact moment we cleared over the stern into the safety of the sea, she rolled over. The *Anhinga* capsized and went under into the abyss. The boat was listing to the port so it would have been much easier to have cleared by swimming off to the lower left side of the cockpit. If we had done the easy thing, she would have rolled over on top of us. If we had not cleared at the very moment we did, we would have been trapped underneath as she rolled and went down. This was a miracle.

The *Anhinga* was gone and we were in the worst possible situation anyone who goes where the ocean is deep could ever be in. We were lost at sea—ninety nautical miles offshore. No one knew anything had happened, and we were in shark-infested waters. I had no doubt in my mind that we were going to die. The ten to twelve nautical miles per hour wind (much faster than anyone can swim) instantly took the fish coolers and poly-balls downwind toward the horizon. Any hope of floatation devices was being blown away before our very eyes. Just then, a small, white, thirty-six-quart Igloo bait cooler came up between Eric and me. We each grabbed a handle with one hand and around each other with the other hand. In that very moment, in perfect unison, without preplanning or discussion we both cried out…

*Our Father, who art in heaven,
hallowed be thy name;
thy kingdom come;
thy will be done;
on earth as it is in heaven.
Give us this day our daily bread.
And forgive us our trespasses,
as we forgive those who trespass against us.
And lead us not into temptation;
but deliver us from evil.
For thine is the kingdom,
the power and the glory,
for ever and ever.
Amen.*

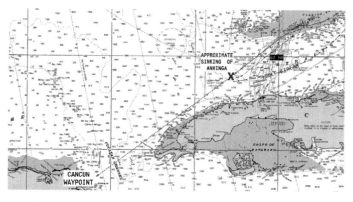

The approximate location of the *Anhinga* when she sank. The NOAA Nautical Chart is historical and not to be used for navigational purposes.

How is it that two men who had never mentioned anything to each other about God or Jesus were praying the Lord's Prayer? We prayed this perfect prayer repeatedly. This is the prayer that Jesus gave us when He was asked how we should pray. To this day, I am still amazed how Eric and I did this with perfect timing, crying out to the Lord in perfect unison. We both had spent enough time on the water to know the odds were not in our favor, and it was going to take a higher power to get us out of this mess.

Please remember this prayer. Sometimes in life, we are filled with a need to pray, but we just do not know what to say. The words aren't there, maybe because our faith is weak, or we're too sad, hurt, ashamed, and lost without a light to set our course. In those times, pray this perfect "Lord's Prayer" from Jesus and listen. Your answer will come in His timing.

Our answer came much quicker than I imagined. As soon as we finished with our rounds of the Lord's Prayer, the *Anhinga* came back up. The overturned hull of the Anhinga came up to the surface with her pair of propellers and rudders rising from a very small section of her hull. She was upside down with just an eight-foot stern section of her bottom about a foot above the water. Thank you, Jesus, for the air trapped in her lazarette, which is the area of bilge below the cockpit deck. We now had something to climb on to get our bodies out of the water. We would no longer be in danger of immediately becoming part of the food chain. We knew we needed to get to the hull for the best odds of survival.

Without having the life raft and the survival kit packed inside it, our ability to survive would be extremely limited. The human body is not designed for prolonged exposure in the sea. Eventually, we would lose too much heat or strength. Unable to hang on, we would slide into the water and drown. That is, if the bull sharks didn't figure out how to get us first. Life rafts are typically yellow or orange to stand out to a would-be rescuer. For now, we were thankful to have the small exposed section of the capsized hull.

Just then, a surfboard popped-up about fifty yards away. It was in a brand-new, shiny, silver travel bag. The importance of the surfboard weighed heavy on my heart. I told Captain Eric that although we needed to get to the hull, I thought I should get that surfboard. As if there was any question about it, we needed things that would float.

In his good-natured manner, he said, "Go ahead, buddy. Go get it."

So I took off in a cross stroke. Arm over arm and taking breaths to get over to where it was, I swam toward it. As I did, the story of how the surfboard came to be on the *Anhinga* flashed through my memory.

Some of the best mates in the world would arrive on the Charter Dock of Sailfish Marina at the end of December for only a handful of jobs. It was Christmas, and I was still in Virginia. I said goodbye to my parents, sister, brother in-law, and very first nephew who had just been born. I would be staying with my Aunt Donna and Uncle Joe at their home in Lake Worth, Florida, which is about forty minutes from Sailfish Marina.

I left Virginia Beach with Neal, Doug, and Andy. Neal and Doug both worked the assembly line building F-150s at Ford Motor Company's Norfolk Assembly Plant. It worked out perfect, the plant was on a two-week maintenance shut down, and I was drained from hunting hard at the end of deer season. Having an extra driver in the truck would be great, so we rode down to Palm Beach together that year.

The six-foot six-inch Wave Riding Vehicles surfboard was a must when it came to personal affects to be packed for the trip down. Mike, my roommate, had given me an old surfboard bag that was a kind of a maroon reddish color on one side and black on the other. Surfboard bags are so important when it comes to protecting the surfboard during travel because the slightest bump can cause a ding or crack in the outer fiberglass. If this happens, water can intrude and saturate the foam, which will destroy the surfboard. The backbone of a surfboard is a thin, quarter-inch, wooden stringer that runs from the tip of the nose to the end of it. It acts as a structural foundation for the board.

Sailfish Marina was the first stop upon arriving in Palm Beach. My friend, Blaine, had helped me get a job on a fifty-one-foot Monterey Sportfish called the *Major Motion* with Captain Jimmy. Little Jimmy may not have been tall in stature, but he was large in heart. Getting to work right away did not leave a whole lot of time to spend with my friends. We did have a few chances to go fishing together, though. At the end of the week, their vacation was over, and it was time for my friends to head back up to Virginia. After they left, I realized my surfboard bag was in the back of Neal's truck.

I knew I wouldn't be able travel to Mexico, Belize, and Guatemala without having a protective travel bag for the surfboard to go in. Prior to the *Anhinga* leaving, I went to the surf shop in Lake Worth and picked through their selection of board bags to find one that had a silver, mylar exterior finish on both sides. Best of all, the bag was on sale, so that's the one I bought.

I was thankful Neal left with the old surfboard bag because the new one was shining like a mirror. While swimming toward the surfboard, I hit something I should have expected—diesel fuel. I don't really remember whether I felt it or smelled it first. I do remember the intense burning on my face and within every little cut on my body. My eyelids seemed to provide little to no protective barrier from the viscous substance as it coated my inner eyelid and eyeball. With only salt water available to flush my eyes, there was no way to relieve the burn. Natural tears were the only help, but each tear was a loss of fluid and one step closer to dehydration.

I hadn't realized there were so many micro-lacerations on my face and body until the fuel entered the cuts with a penetrating sting. It felt like there were fire ants randomly stinging me all over my body.

Trying to breathe while in the diesel fuel coated sea was the most difficult task in the attempt of salvaging the surfboard. When I breathed through my nostrils, the vapors irritated the sensitive tissues lining the nasal cavity and down into my throat. It felt like fire in my nose. I tried breathing through my mouth after the irritation caused my sinuses to close. The taste of the diesel fuel filled it as I was sucking in the vapors. I just wanted the burning to stop. Constantly breathing through my mouth would only dry my throat out more and increase the craving for a drink of water. I attempted to recall what I had learned in college about the health hazards of diesel fuel, but I couldn't remember them.

Oftentimes people ask, "What kind of thoughts go through the mind when a person is in a survival situation?" The primary thought for Captain Eric and I was that there was a job to do. Our job was to survive as long as we could. I was amazed with how the survival instinct affected our thought processes from the moment we went down. The reality was that we would look at a situation, analyze it, and immediately answer the question, "Is this something that could save our lives or not?"

Giving up on getting the surfboard was not an option. I had to force myself to persevere through the pain of the fuel before the surfboard drifted beyond my ability to recover it. Then a critical thought came to mind. *"Dear Lord, please don't let me throw up. I can't afford to lose the food that's in my stomach. I'm gonna need this energy to get me through. Oh please don't let me throw up."*

The struggle to keep from throwing up was real as I continued to swim through that diesel fuel. The urge was intensified by the slime in my eyes and nose. I pressed on through and cleared the fuel to breathe the pure air. At this point, the prize was almost within my reach.

Too often in life, when there's a struggle before us, we want to quit and go the other way. We want to do the easy thing or what's best for our own life at the moment. We cut ourselves short when we don't let the trials that come into our lives finish their work in us. We miss the valuable lesson God plans for our lives. We miss the prize. But in this moment at sea, I made it to the surfboard. I made it to the prize.

Returning to Eric was going to be much easier knowing the solid buoyancy of the surfboard and bag would raise my body out of the water enough for my arm to be the only body part making contact with the fuel. This time, I was going much faster, so I thought maybe I could hold my breath all the way through the diesel slick. I was so excited about this gift that had been provided for Captain Eric and me. I grabbed a rail on each side of the surfboard, and with a strong kick, my body leaped out of the water and onto the board like I had done so many times before.

When making the very first stroke back toward Eric, I immediately noticed that something did not feel right. I had never paddled a surfboard in its protective bag before, but

I still didn't think it should feel the way it did. *Why does it feel less buoyant? Why is it so unstable?* The thoughts of the surfboard were quickly pushed aside as I needed to get back to my captain.

I set the nose of the surfboard on course to returning across the diesel fuel slick to where I had left Eric. With one trial resolved, another manifested. Where was the *Anhinga*? And of greater concern, where was Eric?

CHAPTER 4:

HIGH HOPES FOR THE EPIRB

My back was arched to its limit to get my chest as high off the surfboard as possible while passing back through the diesel. My concern for Captain Eric certainly outweighed the stings and burns of the fuel as I made my way toward his last known location. After passing through the fuel, there he was. Thank Jesus he had not been caught under the shaft or in the propellers. There was my captain, treading water with his sunglasses and ball cap on. His face displayed confidence we would make it through this. I made my way back to him, but the *Anhinga* was gone, and we would never see her again.

The *Anhinga* was off to the crushing depths of the abyss, which was about five-thousand-feet below Eric and I. She was probably being carried in an easterly direction by the Gulf Stream as she was sinking. The pressure would be increasing by one atmosphere for every thirty-three feet she went down. I imagined how air pockets were imploding as the pressure increased. Piece by piece, the *Anhinga* was breaking apart. The beautifully handcrafted vessel would soon be a shipwreck, her parts becoming a new home for the eels and other bottom feeders.

Other than pieces of the boat from around areas where the *Anhinga* broke apart, there wasn't a lot of debris around us. The items on deck were blown out of our sight by the light breeze. The lack of any kind of background noise enhanced the solidarity of our situation. We were alone at sea, and no one knew. Eric and I never said the words because we didn't have to. The reality of the situation was setting in. A part of me hoped I was still asleep and this was some sort of nightmare. This was no dream at all. This was really happening. We needed to find the emergency position indicating radio beacon. We knew it was out there somewhere in the beautiful deep blue sea.

My thoughts quickly returned to the very thing Eric and I were hanging on to. I wondered, *What's wrong with the surfboard? This board stood up to some big waves when Trick and I were in California. There isn't enough extra space inside the board bag for it to be floating around in there.* It's a strong board with a solid spine. With my hands pressing on the bottom of the board bag, I discreetly performed a head-to-toe check with the same determination as a paramedic with a patient. The process quickly revealed the impact of the rogue wave had broken the board. I didn't know how bad it was, but this was certainly not the time to tell Eric. The purpose of the foam in a surfboard is buoyancy, and it was becoming saturated.

The sea surface was fairly slick looking as the two to three-foot swells rolled past. As time went on, the glassy sea surface was penetrated by pieces of debris. The debris was slowly rising and breaking the surface like the turtles popping up in my neighbor's pond. The debris was becoming scattered everywhere. All of it was in small pieces.

The largest piece of the *Anhinga* I ever found was an eight-foot section of her shear. The section was part of her starboard side from below the aft window, down and out along the deck. The piece was constructed of laminated plywood with several layers of fiberglass and an exterior finish of baby blue paint. A piece of standard electrical wiring was stapled to the interior side of the plywood. I thought, *Wow, we could really use this. We might be able to use this to tie things together.* I pulled with all my might to break that wire loose, but it would not break free. The staples holding it in place were just too strong for me to to pull it free while being in the water. My effort resulted in failure.

Even though Captain Eric and I were there together, it was extremely lonely floating with the thoughts of doom rolling over and over in my head. The sun was getting a little higher and brighter. Many watermen know that with the sun burning off the morning chill, the wind can start to blow. The breeze did begin to start blowing harder with the sun.

We had been in the water for over an hour. The morning chill had retreated from the air, but it had remained in our bones. The thoughts I had were relatively insignificant for me at the time, but as my body started to get a little cold, I started to reflect, *Is Eric chillier than I am? I hope he's all right. If only I had a pair of sunglasses. I would trade a shotgun for a pair of sunglasses.* I needed to distract my mind from going down a negative thought pattern, so I started to sing that well-known hymn by Charlotte Elliott, "Just as I Am without One Plea."

> Just as I am, without one plea
> But that Thy blood was shed for me
> And that Thou bid'st me come to Thee
> O Lamb of God, I come! I come
> Just as I am, with many a conflict, many a doubt...

Dag-gum, my singing sucks. I hope God isn't cringing as He hears this. It sure is a good thing He listens more to the sound of our hearts than my off key, tone deafness. Hound dogs can sing better than I can. "Hear my heart O Lord and rescue us."

The wind had picked up, and more debris from the *Anhinga* was rising to the surface as she sank into the crushing pressures of the abyss. In the debris, Eric was able to find a half-inch thick plywood engine hatch cover with a boarder framed out of two-by-two boards on the bottom. The cover was approximately five-feet long by three-feet wide. It was something to hang on to. The smaller pieces of debris did not have enough structural integrity to even slightly get our shoulders out of the water.

The reality that Eric and I did not speak of was if we didn't find the EPIRB, we would probably die. With the discovery of the engine cover, he now had something to float on. I had to save my captain. I had to go out to find the emergency beacon, life raft, or anything else that might help to save our lives. Looking down the sea, splintered fragments of wood and baby blue painted debris from the *Anhinga* were forming a trash line. I looked at Captain Eric and asked for permission to go out on the search. He graciously granted permission.

Often when people go to the beach, they stand on the shore and admire the beauty of a singular massive body of water stretching from one continent to another. Fishermen see something different. We see multiple bodies of water within the same massive body. Our eyes are conditioned to look for the slightest difference in surface ripples or even color and clarity. These "changes," as we call them, can be the difference between coming home with a skunk in the fish box, a zero, or stacking the dock with a load of fish to earn hero status. Sometimes when two different bodies of water meet, floating debris will meet up and push together in a line as the current edges collide. The line is often made up of macroalgae called sargassum seaweed mixed with trash. This trash came from little red buckets, US Navy drones, square grouper, refrigerators, or rafts that once belonged to escaping refuges who are no more.

I asked Eric for permission to use the surfboard to go looking for the EPIRB. Once again, he replied with his gentle and kind Australian accent, "Okay, go ahead buddy." I situated myself on the surfboard with my back arched as I had been taught by Wes, an ex-professional surfer. The knowledge I had gained in exchange for a fish story was really coming in handy.

I pointed the surfboard in the direction of the trash line, and then I reached out my right arm as far as I could with my hand cupped and dug into the blue sea to begin the sluggish move forward. The broken surfboard was still in the bag. Surfboards are typically made with two pieces of foam that have been laminated side by side, shaped, and covered with fiberglass. A more detailed inspection of the surfboard discovered this affected both sides of the surfboard; therefore, the board was slowly becoming more saturated with water.

The trash line was straight as it extended down sea. It was mostly made up of small pieces of wooden debris from the construction of the boat's hull, house, deck, and interior. The exterior was obvious by the light blue paint. It was almost like a game trying to figure out where each piece of flotsam may have come from. I was scanning the entire line trying to focus on each individual piece as I passed. Looking big for a trained eye to notice something small seemed to be the best option for finding an object close to the size of a small two-and-a-half-pound kitchen fire extinguisher. The ocean is a big place to cover when trying to find fish. While filling in as a mate on the *American Lady* with Captain Joey, I was taught to look out just below the horizon at four miles and my eye would naturally catch a single fish breaking between the boat and the distant point.

I wondered if my buddies running their charter fishing trips out of the Hatteras Island and Oregon Inlet would be fishing this trash line, making their customers happy and filling the fish box with mahi long after our bodies had decomposed with our bones scattered on the ocean floor.

There was so much debris it looked like an image you'd see on the news after an EF4 tornado passed through a mobile home park. Splinters of wood and other construction materials created a surreal feeling of impending doom. To think, this vessel designed and built to carry us on safe passage was instantly destroyed by the mighty power of the sea. The debris line of the *Anhinga* seemed as if it was alive, like a gigantic eel, as the material moved in the passing swells. The material was moving in sequence as each of the swells passed by, like a crowd performing "the wave" in a stadium. This collective trash line gave high hopes for locating some of the life safety equipment.

This trash line was a blessing. I could not imagine how difficult the search process would be if the debris was scattered all over the surface of the Gulf Stream. The rapidly forming line provided a solid indication we were located in a strong converging current. Finding the EPIRB was like finding a single four-leaf clover in a fifty-acre field of seed drilled cover. That is, if the four-leaf clover even existed in the field. We knew the EPRIB was somewhere, but we wouldn't know if it had made it out of the *Anhinga* unless we found it.

It was still so surreal to think it was the *Anhinga* that I was following. On any average day of charter fishing, we search the ocean looking for a line of sea grass or some other sort of trash because on that edge is where the fish congregate. The last time I traveled along a line of debris, it was while looking for the colorful and tasty mahi that were feeding on minnows. I wondered how long it would take for the food chain to start to build in the deep blue sea below. I tried not to look straight down so I wouldn't think about it. The fastening staples protruding from the pieces of laminate were probably the worst part of paddling or swimming through the debris. They were constantly cutting and scratching my face and arms, which allowed the salt water to enter my body and burn. I was too focused on finding the EPRIB or life raft to worry about this minor discomfort. The reality was each of the little cuts were probably leaving droplets of blood in the water.

As I searched, I couldn't help but think this wasn't the first time God had come knocking on my door, trying to get my attention. It happened during the summer of 1994, when a Bermuda high pressure system set in over the Eastern Mid-Atlantic States. The heat was unbearable to the point that no average summertime cold front could penetrate or move it. This meant long stretches of sixteen- to seventeen-hour workdays, seven days a week. On a long streak of working every day, a mate's prayer might go sort of like this: "God, please make this thing break down, but not too bad. Nothing that is expensive or can keep us down for more than a couple days."

On the *High Hopes*, we had fished for a couple months straight without a day off. They were tough days. To put this into perspective, a mate could work 1,155 hours in a couple months where the average worker would have that many hours in just under seven months. The high-pressure system made it sticky and hot with the only breeze during the middle of the day being the wind at whatever the speed of the boat was at the time.

Another condition resulting from this weather system was stagnant water. The lack of wind, especially easterly winds, does not generate the desired currents to feed the edge or push new water up onto the continental shelf off the East Coast.

Those were the kind of days where the charter stares at you all day long like it's your fault there are hardly any fish in the box.

Captain David Wright and me after good day of white marlin fishing aboard the *High Hopes* out of Rudee Inlet. Many years ago, he noticed Captain Omie Tillett was on the radio, praying over the Oregon Inlet fleet on the way out every morning. It was put on Captain Dave's heart to do the same for the Rudee Inlet fleet. He still does.

Captain Dave always joked about a monster he called the Gillman. Sometimes, we would see a monster out there like the one in the movie *The Creature from the Black Lagoon*. It would stick its head straight up from the water while we were fishing out there on the rip. It only happened when we were deliriously tired. Really, there was a sea monster-looking thing that always seemed to raise its head out of the water right about the time one of us was about to doze off. Our monsters were leather-back sea turtles, so ugly they had a face only a mother could love—maybe!

The last daily task during the day's fishing trip was repairing any tackle or gear that was damaged. I clocked out on the seventeenth hour of that day with everything prepped for the next day's charter. I sat down in a barrel chair to take a brief rest before heading to the parking lot. An hour later, I woke up and realized there was no possible way I'd have time to party that night. So, I jumped in my lifted Ford Ranger for the forty-minute drive home to the rural south end of Virginia Beach. It was one of those kinds of rides with music and air conditioning blasting to help stay awake.

Pungo Ferry is an unforgiving two-lane road spanning across the Intercoastal Waterway and the adjacent swamp. It is just shy of three miles long with a church and house on the east end and a couple houses on the west end. The road's unforgiveness is due to what appears to be wide shoulders that is really nothing more than grass growing on swamp mud. So, the second a tire leaves the road, the swamp sucks the vehicle in. On the other hand, that's a good thing because a car sinking into the swamp usually slowed the speeding vehicle down before striking one of the cypress trees beside the shoulder. The swamp had claimed many vehicles, including our family car when my sister was behind the wheel.

The high-rise bridge portion of the road is a little more forgiving with its four- or five-foot wide solid shoulder. The Pungo Ferry Bridge is a fixed bridge that is about seventy feet tall to allow for boats to travel three thousand miles from Boston, Massachusetts, to the southern tip of Florida. Captain George's Seafood Restaurant sat at the dead-end of the old ferry road. This restaurant had employed many of the county kids over the years, and the parking lot being on the water made it a late-night hangout spot.

The last thing I remember was the right turn onto Pungo Ferry Road. My body finally said, "You are done," and I blacked out. Somehow, I had managed to make it up the bridge about three-quarters of a mile down the road. I must have been going at a pretty good speed. When the lifted Ranger drifted over, the front passenger tire climbed right up and above the right-side wall.

I came to just in time to see the truck go vertical and the front tire clip the light pole about a foot above the top of the wall. Thankfully, when the tire hit the pole, it forced the truck back toward the bridge. It landed on the driver's side and slid across the bridge to the left wall. I remember being pinned back in the seat with my seat belt on with my right hand pushing on the roof while my left hand was on the a-pillar with my left elbow dragging on the road. There was smoke in the air but not so much that I couldn't see what was getting ready to happen. The top of the cab was about to strike the other wall with extreme force. I remember thinking, *I'm going to die.* But just before the impact, it was like there was a gentle push off the wall and the truck slowly made a quarter turn and stopped in the middle of the road.

Now, I certainly didn't take time to ponder the miracle that had just happened. Why? Because I saw smoke, smelled smoke, saw sparks, and thought, *She's going to blow!* I had never moved so fast in my life. I don't have any idea how I climbed up and out the passenger door so fast, but it didn't matter because I was out of that thing.

Little did I know, my friend Arbee happened to be on the front porch of Captain George's watching the whole thing happen. Arbee was the first person to arrive on the scene, and he informed me it looked like a fireball going over the bridge. It sure was comforting to see him. Fortuitous too, since Arbee was a deputy with the Virginia Beach Sheriff's Department. So when the police arrived, he explained I was a charter boat mate who had worked most of the summer without a day off. He also greeted my parents when they crested the bridge to see the Ranger totaled in the middle of the road. Thank God I hadn't been partying that night! At that time, I was the mate on the biggest and most booked charter boat in Virginia. I chased fish all day and the ladies most of the night. Ego and pride were ruling my life.

The next day at 4:15 a.m., I was back at the boat with a bandaged arm, ready to go fishing. When Captain Dave heard the story of what happened, he said, "I'll find somebody to cover. You aren't fishing today." I had finally gotten my coveted day off. Mates do not like to take a day off if the boat is still fishing because they might miss out on catching a blue marlin. So naturally, they caught a blue marlin that day.

This wasn't the first time the job had almost killed me, but this time something supernatural intervened. It started to sink in that I had just experienced a miracle. God had saved my life, but why? You would think this might be enough to give cause for a change in my lifestyle, but that's another story.

As I treaded water in the wake of the remains of the *Anhinga*, I wondered if God would once again save me. I searched and searched the debris knowing well what the life raft looked like. Unfortunately, I had failed to get a good description of the ditch bag. Ditch bags usually have a distinct international orange, yellow, or red color to be recognized as safety equipment. The ironic thing is most of the mako sharks I have caught over the years were on a rig of these same colors. The bags typically include items such as critical medications, a handheld VHF radio, a knife, twine, a waterproof light source, food, water, maybe some recently expired or extra flares, and so on. The *Anhinga*'s ditch bag contained the EPRIB. I wished I'd paid more attention to what the ditch bag looked like as I stepped around the life raft in the salon. I felt like a failure.

I continued to stalk the line as I paddled down sea and reached the next dilemma. I'd come to a fork in the debris where one line continued down sea while the other extended off at forty-five degrees to my left. People often use the term "fork in the road" to represent choices in life. For me, this was a choice of life or death. There was no question in my choice to accept Jesus. It was a choice of life, and I hoped He would help me make the right choices while trying to survive.

I did not have the luxury of taking a chance on one line or the other. Both lines had to be searched.

Paddling a surfboard is like paddling a canoe from the front seat. I wanted to travel down the diagonal line to my left, so I paddled with several back-to-back strokes with my right arm. With forward momentum, the nose of the board gracefully came around to match the angle of the diagonal debris line. I could not help but notice the slightly glassy sea surface conditions were yielding to the breeze as the entire surface became covered in ripples. The wind direction was meeting the swell direction at its side. I had seen the evolution of a dangerous sea state enough to know that I did not like the symptoms the Gulf Stream was starting to show. I knew it was going to get nasty within the next several hours.

CHAPTER 5:

JUST ONE MORE PICTURE

The sea and atmospheric conditions certainly started to change. I could feel the pressure dropping. The swells were now making contact with the rear-to-rear quarter of the surfboard as they passed by. The wind was picking up. This increased the need for me to make quick work of searching the diagonal line. Upon reaching the end of the diagonal debris line, I turned and traveled back up the other side until reaching the main line again. I had wasted energy searching the diagonal line of debris. I had nothing to show for my efforts. Not only had I failed again, but I lacked a certain confidence in the quality of my effort. I had allowed my fear of losing the main line of debris distract me from my task of salvation. Following the main line was the only way to get back to Captain Eric.

I brought the nose of the surfboard around to continue on the down sea course along the main line of debris. With each stroke, I continued to inspect the debris for any items of importance or scraps of treasure offering some sort of hope for our rescue. I had probably paddled out nearly a thousand yards before reaching the end of the down sea line of debris.

The time had come for me to go back to Captain Eric and provide him with the report of my failure once again. The line was still holding together fairly tight, providing an easy path for my return voyage. I had a more thorough and slower inspection of the line while paddling up-sea. There was a slight pushback on the surfboard as I met each wave advancing toward me. I was making headway while being able to see through the swells and into the water a little easier than when on the down sea search.

I had to fill my mind with positive thoughts about the up-sea paddle to overcome the feelings of failure for not finding the EPIRB or life raft. Plus, the deteriorating condition of the surfboard was exponentially noticeable as I paddled into the rougher conditions associated with paddling up-sea. I hoped it would continue to maintain some of its buoyancy through the night. I had to redirect my thoughts toward analyzing value of each piece of debris. Was it lifesaving?

Sometimes, we take the simple things in life for granted. The items we typically see as waste most days could be critical to survival the next. It was around noon when I was paddling back toward Eric, and I started to get thirsty. The last time I had something to drink was seven hours prior with my bagel supreme. I reflected on the many times I had brushed my teeth and allowed the precious freshwater to keep running out of the faucet. So many times, I had stood in the shower meditating as the fresh water flowed in an endless stream out of the showerhead and down the drain. Or, I stood mesmerized as the fresh water passed through the hose and jetted out of the nozzle in an arch only to wastefully land on the ground. If only I could have that one sip of clear, fresh water left in the bottom of the hundreds of un-empty bottles I had thrown in the trash can.

I was raised better than to be wasteful. This characteristic had been passed down from my grandmother and her two sisters, Ruth and Martha (Ann), who had received it from their grandfather. I will never forget the look of pain in the eyes of my Great Aunt Ruth when she described the struggle our family and many other southern families had endured during the Reconstruction period after the Civil War. They were hard times when there were little to no resources. I think that's why the three sisters recycled everything from Christmas wrapping paper to aluminum foil.

I continued to scan the waters looking for a bottle of water or anything that could serve purposefully toward our survival. The sea conditions were not allowing the gathering of items to be easy. Captain Eric and I needed some sort of bag or sack to store any beneficial pieces of the *Anhinga*'s trash line we might find floating around us. Any piece of life-preserving trash would do. In this moment, trash was more valuable than precious stones or gold. After all, what good would all of the precious stones and gold in the world be to us now? They'd do nothing but weigh us down and sink us. I wondered if Eric had found anything of value while I had been out searching the line.

My eyes fixed on a whitish object floating just below the surface. The unidentified floating object flowed with the motion of the water. As I approached the object, I could see it was a plastic grocery bag. When I reached out my hand, I discovered the grocery bag was filled with some of the finest fillet mignon I had ever seen. It was a gift. I untied the bag and quickly dumped out the contents. The gift was not the contents of fine steaks, but the half-a-cent bag they were packed in. We had no way to cook raw, bloody meat, which was really expensive shark bait.

Finally, we had a way to retain whatever resources we found without fear of a wave breaking on us and losing everything. I was amazed how something as seemingly insignificant as a grocery bag could bring so much hope and completeness. The real hope was in the next step of finding something to put in the bag. Hydration and nourishment were the priority for our little half-a-cent plastic bag.

As I paddled back up the line, I noticed something yellow floating in the water. The item looked like some sort of storage bag. The closer I approached, the sharper the contrast became between the tropical blue sea and the bright yellow bag. Soon, I recognized what it was—one of my prized possessions that had been purchased specifically for fishing pictures: my thirty-five-millimeter underwater Minolta camera. The pictures from the previous year were taken with a waterproof disposable camera. The quality of the images had been so poor, people looked like Smurfs—as blue as the water.

Prior to the summer of 1997, Captain Dave and I both bought a Minolta Weathermatic 35DL. These cameras took wonderful, crisp pictures above and below the water. The camera had not been used very much while I was charter fishing out of Sailfish Marina, but the lost time was made up for in the Bahamas with Eric and the boss's family.

I paddled up to the camera, reached out, and grabbed the black strap. I unzipped the top to expose its contents. I became irrationally excited and thankful for such a wonderful gift, as if there would be a bottle of water or a candy bar inside, but there wasn't. Inside the bag, there were several watertight film canisters. Some had new rolls of film and others had used rolls that were waiting to be developed. My trip in the Bahamas was one of them. *Why did I bring them? I thought. I should have left them with the rest of my stuff at Aunt Donna and Uncle Joe's place. Where could I have had them developed in the middle of a jungle? It was a waste to bring them on this trip.*

I removed the camera from the bag. Bobbing in the water, I kicked around in a circle snapping pictures. For some reason, I felt it was necessary to build a panorama of the destruction all around me. At this point, I knew I was going to die. It was just going to be a matter of time. I guess I felt the need to take the pictures to let my family, my friends, and the world know what happened in my last hours of life.

I hoped someone would eventually find the camera and develop the film to see the final story of the crew of the *Anhinga*, lost in the Gulf Stream.

I wondered how much farther away Eric was. I wonder if anyone ever found that thirty-five-millimeter camera.

The *Anhinga* leaving the slip at Sailfish Marina, Stuart, Florida.

CHAPTER 6:

IMPULSIVE HOPE

Our fate now burned into thirty-five-millimeter film, I turned the nose of the surfboard up-sea once more, leaving behind the last record of the crew of the *Anhinga*. One stroke at a time, I was making my way back toward Captain Eric. As I did, a nagging thought about the trash line burned in my brain. I realized there were some items floating in the line I surely had not seen on the trip out, items that must still have been rising to the surface from the depths of the abyss. I wondered if the EPIRB had surfaced somewhere in the line after I had passed.

I began to notice a pattern in debris based on where items were stored on the boat. Things located near each other and of similar densities were floating near each other in the line of debris. If I could find cushions from inside the salon, the EPRIB could be close by. I tried to recall a picture in my mind of the route searched. *Had I seen anything from the salon?*

After passing the diagonal line, I knew I was getting closer to Captain Eric. The fatigue was setting in from all of the energy expended on my failed mission. The white paint on the rectangular engine hatch was fairly easy to spot from a distance as my eyes fixed on Eric. Something looked different around him. I wondered what he had found. There was something white and orange. *Whatever it is, it's making his footprint look larger in the sea, perfect to help get the attention of a rescue plane.*

The new additions became clear as I closed the distance between us. The Lord had provided more gifts in our time of need. Captain Eric was wearing one of our backup life jackets for cruising in the Intercoastal Waterway. The life jacket was a Type II, which has an intended use for ponds for day cruising on inland waters near the shoreline. Basically, they were for use on a small lake where the wearer can easily make it to shore or if the chance of rescue is immediate. Type II devices are not designed for stress of rough, offshore waters, while Type I personal flotation devices are designed for offshore conditions and provide the greatest buoyancy. I couldn't help but to give praise as I came near Eric. "Thank you, Jesus. I was so afraid, not knowing how long he would have the strength to hang on as the wind increased."

Eric had also been able to acquire a bench-seat cushion from the flybridge. The cushion had some age on it and was made with a fairly thin layer of foam. It was another item that was not very buoyant, but we could use it to wrap around the hard edges of the plywood. Eric was making his best attempt to use the cushion as a shield between himself and the engine hatch, but there was no way to secure the two together. If we only had some rope, we could've tied them together. There was a lot of rope on the *Anhinga* when she went down. A simple roll of string was all we needed.

My feeling of being a failure grew as I approached Captain Eric. I was dreading giving him the report that was obvious. "Cap, I couldn't find the EPIRB or the life raft. I'm sorry."

"That's all right," Eric assured me. "They'll turn up, or someone will find us."

I still had not been able to shake away the feeling of being a failure when Eric and I noticed something orange floating about forty yards away. The object made a spin with the passing of the next wave. It was another Type II life jacket. I left the surfboard and quickly swam over to grab the life jacket and put it on. I wondered where the flare kits were.

Upon my return, I noticed Eric looked like he was in a little pain.

"Hanging onto that thing looks really uncomfortable," I said to him. "Do you want to switch?"

If I didn't know any better, I'd say even his laughter had an Australian accent. He replied through a chuckle. "Yes, I would love to switch."

I still had not mentioned anything about the surfboard being broken in the bag. I also did not say a word about finding my camera and taking pictures. If I would have told Eric, he would have known the camera being left behind was my sign of having no hope in rescue. We chatted for a little while about our hope in rescue and how it might come to be.

A short while later, my theory about items of similar buoyancy in the same location on the boat was proven to be true. The two Orion flare canisters we had onboard the *Anhinga* were stored next to the life jackets on the bridge. The life jackets and the flare canisters were just another example of how God gave little blessings at just the right time. He lifted our spirits to give us hope in a hopeless situation.

Eric and I were alone, just floating in the debris with thoughts rolling over in our minds. The kind of thoughts we did not want to talk about. While floating, we both stood watch for the highly unlikely rescuer in a boat or a plane.

Either one of them would do. We came up with a plan to keep lookout. Eric would use his hat to shade his eyes as he kept an eye on the horizon to watch for a boat. I would lay back and use his sunglasses to pan the sky for an airplane. If we spotted one, we would use the flares to signal them and the nightmare would be over. This was an awesome plan.

During the idle time, there were also pleasant thoughts. Like remembering the first time I ever saw the beautiful Gulf Stream water. It was so deep blue that it almost had a hint of purple to it. My first job on an offshore charter boat was on the *Impulsive*, a forty-three-foot Sonny Briggs built in Wanchese, North Carolina. Captain Kenny had recently gotten his license and had been a mate for some very well-respected fishermen, so I figured he was a great one to learn from. He was. On my trip as a mate out of Oregon Inlet, Kenny yelled for me to come up on the bridge.

I climbed the ladder. "Yes, sir, Cap."

He said, "Do you see those clouds up there in front of us that look like popcorn?"

"Yes, sir," I replied.

"That's the Gulf Stream, so we're getting close to the temperature change. Get the baits ready."

The same Gulf Stream where I saw the popcorn clouds for the first time was about eight hundred and fifty miles north-northeast from where I was now floating. *Will our bodies make it that far?* These unique clouds were as beautiful then as the first day I had ever seen them. I only wish I would see a plane flying below them. *I'll never see Kenny again. I wish I could tell him goodbye.*

The good thing about looking up in the sky is you can't look up and down at same time. In the Mid-Atlantic states of the East Coast, it seems to be easier to gain a perspective of the depth of outer space on a clear night with a northwesterly wind. The drier air just seems to be so clear with the sky continuing out to infinity. During the daylight, the sky seems to be a little less vast with the same atmospheric conditions.

The ocean is the opposite. At night, the seawater seems to quickly absorb available light, so it's hard to see deeper than several feet. In crystal clear blue water during the daylight, the water seems to go continuously down into the dark of the abyss. The depths of the oceans are still a thing of great mystery. Of course, our charts and depth sounders/bottom machines provide verification the depths are not limitless.

But fears of the creatures lurking in the sea below Eric and I now could have easily been limitless. There was so much depth potential for a predator to be below us. I was very thankful to have the easy job of watching the sky, reducing the likelihood of accidently looking down into the depths. Like tightrope walkers, we avoided looking down. We figured it was best to keep the cycle of fearful thoughts at bay. There was no point in adding additional fear. We did not have time for that. Survival was our mission.

I only recall looking down into the depths a few times throughout the entire struggle. There was so much of God's beauty seen from the horizon to the sky. Just as we train our eyes to pick up on the slightest difference in sea surface current features, we fishermen also train our eyes to identify shapes, colors, and shadows just below the surface of the water. There was a split-second flash below the surface, which brought my attention down into the blue Gulf Stream water.

In an instant, a small school of dolphinfish or mahi-mahi was below us. The three-foot fish were darting with quick, sharp, precise maneuvers as they hunted for and pursued their next meal among the debris line of the *Anhinga*. They had the same agility as an F-18 Super Hornet being pursued by an enemy missile through a twisting and curving mountain pass. It reminded me of a scene in the film *Behind Enemy Lines*, where Lieutenant Chris Burnett is attempting to outrun and maneuver the surface to air missiles that were fired at his aircraft.

The mahi were a blessing. I had a brief moment of thought about the fact that smaller fish are often pursued by larger fish or sharks. In the offshore pelagic fish world, a three-foot fish is far from being a tier one predator. The thought of a marlin pursuing the mahi did not worry me, but the thought of sharks did. The fear was quickly overcome with the peace of seeing the creatures' beautiful combination of colors. The array of blues, yellows, greens, and silvers to white was an assurance there is a Creator who loves us enough to provide such an amazing fish. The fish can reach speeds of sixty miles per hour and is one of the fastest-growing fish in the ocean. As quickly as they arrived, they were gone. The schools of mahi had saved the day on many charters and had put a lot of money in my pocket over the years.

I often wonder if they stayed near us throughout the day. Catching glimpses of them was amazing. Fish swimming in the water are much easier to spot from high in the tuna tower and become increasingly more difficult at the level of the cockpit deck. With our heads at the sea surface, it was very difficult to see down into the water unless we looked straight down. This was one time it was good not to have the advantage of height like in the top of a tuna tower. We did not want to know what else was down there.

The brief distraction from the mission of panning the skies for a potential rescuer was over. It was time to get back to work watching for a plane to signal. I thought about all the times I flew back and forth between Norfolk International and Palm Beach International airports. There had been many times when I had the window seat. I enjoyed peering out of the face-sized oval hole with a fixation on the diagonal lines of the waves as boats traveled by, wondering where their destinations were.

The boats had been whitish specs on the surface of the Atlantic. The rougher the sea conditions were, the harder it was to identify an object below. The lines of waves were easily recognizable, especially when their angle changes as they get closer to shore until they're running almost parallel. The whitecaps are also a pretty good indicator of the sea conditions. I wondered if a person in the water could be seen from that elevation. I was probably the only one on the plane having thoughts even close to this.

If we were to see a plane, I hoped it would be a passenger plane rather than a plane carrying cargo. Passenger planes have a lot of people sitting in the window seats, and maybe there'd be just one with an interest in watching the sea below. A passenger might possibly look down to see a faint cloud of orange smoke and bring it to the attention of a flight attendant. The flight attendant could get to the captain of the plane in time to get a fix on our location to relay it to the Coast Guard. If only we could see a plane.

As we floated there, bobbing up and down on the four-foot waves, Eric was still panning the horizon and I was still watching the sky. I prayed for a miracle. "Please Lord, send a plane we can signal for our rescue." I wanted to walk through those doors of Blackwater Baptist and see the painting of Jesus. Prior to being nailed to the cross, Jesus went out to pray while at Gethsemane. In his prayer he said, "*Abba*, Father... everything is possible for you. Take this cup from me. Yet not what I will, but what you will" (Mark 14:36 ESV). Eric and I wanted to be rescued. We wanted this cup taken away.

Shortly after the prayer, there it was. It was a plane! It was high, but we could see the whole shape with the beautiful blue sky as a backdrop. The plane was probably up at thirty or forty thousand feet.

Eric and I quickly sprang into action. The O-ring seal in the middle of the barrel-like Orion flare canister was released by twisting the recessed handles at each end. The top half of the international orange canister was removed to expose the contents of a single twenty-five-millimeter flare pistol with a bandolier holding four signal bullets, three handheld red flare signals, a handheld orange smoke signal, a whistle, a palm-sized handheld signal mirror, and a three-foot square distress flag.

The plane would have been out of sight in the time required to remove the protective sticker on the signal mirror. The ten-inch long, handheld, orange smoke signal was the best option to create an orange mass to drift downwind, making a larger presence for the passengers to see. I grasped the base of the rod-shaped device with my left hand and twisted off the cap on top with my right hand, exposing the smoke ignition material on the tip of the signal. Next, the black cover was flipped off the removed cap to expose the striker.

This was the moment we had been praying for. It was time to activate the signal to save our lives. I kicked hard with my feet to elevate my body as much as possible to have a good strike to ignite the smoke. A right-handed glancing blow was struck across the igniter of the flare with the coarse surface exposed on the cap. The attempt failed. I tried again and it failed. The third attempt worked. We had ignition! Eric had been more successful with his attempt lighting his flare. A large plume of orange smoke erupted across the surface of the water. I laid back in the water, now holding the flare extended upward with my right arm. The smoke poured out for about a minute.

Someone must be looking out of the window and seeing this. Better get another flare ready. It was only a matter of time before we would see the plane start to bank to the right and drop her nose for the pilots to verify the information the flight attendants had just reported to them. Surely, God had answered our prayers, and only a few hours into the ordeal!

Our smoke had laid a good signal perpendicular to the windows, so why wasn't the plane altering course? It was continuing away from us. We failed to alert the passengers of the plane that there were Americans in peril in the sea below them. I couldn't help but shout in my mind, *God, did you hear the prayer for rescue? Did you hear our prayer not to die?*

I was angry.

The airplane passing us was a significant moment of a high and a low. A feeling of extreme excitement followed by intense failure and depression. This was another hash mark on my list of failures in a time when failure was unacceptable. This should have saved us. I was so certain.

I felt responsible even though there was no blame to be had. This was the beginning of many highs and lows to come throughout the day. Another failure occurred as a result of my effort to reseal the flare container after attempting to signal the plane. The top half of the orange canister was placed over the bottom. Grabbing the end handles, I pressed the two halves together, creating pressure to get the O-ring to reseal as I twisted the halves until they locked together with a snap. The canister must have later bumped into something as a swell passed, causing the canister to open and our twenty-five-millimeter pistol to sink into the abyss.

Captain Eric and I resumed our lookout positions with him watching the sea surface and me watching the sky. I floated on my back with my left arm stretched out across the engine hatch and right arm across the bench-seat cushion. I was thankful we were in the tropical water of the Gulf Stream. The tropical water is denser because of the higher salinity, which makes it easier for human bodies to float.

I could not keep myself from reflecting on the latest failure. *The airplane was the perfect opportunity for our rescue. If only I could have found the EPRIB, the plane would have picked up the distress signal. They would have circled around, dropped down, and waved their wings as they went by on a low pass. The United States Coast Guard would have a C-130 airplane here within an hour with a survival drop.*

Captain Eric and I tried to bolster our spirits with occasional small talk as we floated. Then, I heard Eric say, "There is a white spec on the horizon."

My father took me out deep-sea fishing for the first time on a head boat out of Boynton Inlet while we were in Palm Beach, Florida. On that day, I told Mom and Dad I was going to work on a fishing boat, while holding a bonito.

CHAPTER 7:

A SPECK ON THE HORIZON

I scanned frantically for the white spec Captain Eric had spotted. What was it? More importantly, where was it going? Had it already passed us?

Was this spec on the horizon our salvation? The white object was certainly some sort of vessel. It was so beautiful to see as it was surrounded in blues. The partly cloudy sky collided with the aquamarine of the tropical water to form the beautiful backdrop it passed through.

I prayed with everything in my soul for God to send us a rescuer. The prayers were so intense, it felt like everything on both sides of my diaphragm were turning inside out. I could literally feel it in my heart, gut, and lungs. So often as a kid, I had heard "God hears your prayers" from my Sunday school teacher. I heard the preacher tell us from the pulpit of Blackwater Baptist Church to "trust in God" and how "He hears your prayers." I had retained little from sitting in the pews other than the accurate count of ceiling tiles in the sanctuary.

I thought the airplane that had passed us earlier was the answer to my prayer, but it hadn't been. We were so afraid to be too positive about the spec that neither Eric nor I mentioned a thing about it being a potential rescue. Possibly he was thinking the same thing I was about the previous disappointment. After all, the plane was almost directly above us. The worst case for us would have been for the spec to get smaller.

With our emotions in reserve, we continued to watch with great hope this would be our rescuer. The object grew in size until it started to look like a rectangular prism. It was still many miles away as we watched the object grow in length, but we knew it would be going broadside past us. We could only hope it would be within range to see our flares. The shape became more defined as it got closer. We could now see it was a ship, but what kind of ship? Its white color made me think it might be a US Naval Hospital Ship. *Maybe it's the* Comfort *or* Mercy?

The *USNS Comfort* and *Mercy* are hospital ships owned by the US Navy. The *Comfort*'s home port is the Norfolk Naval Station. Encounters with the Naval ships stationed at the Norfolk Naval Station are a common sight when fishing out of Virginia Beach. We had to cross the shipping lanes that lead into the Chesapeake Bay on the way to and from the offshore fishing grounds. The Navy's ships and submarines use this shipping lane when leaving and returning to the Norfolk Naval Base. Naval Station Norfolk is the largest in the world.

Ships can often be seen performing practice exercises on the offshore fishing ground. Communication between the Navy and our charter fishing fleet is essential to maintaining safety. The Navy has always been great to work with. There have been many occasions when the Navy was already performing drills in the morning when the fishing fleet arrived to the fishing grounds on the continental shelf just south of the Norfolk Canyon. If the location was the only hot spot where the fish had congregated, often the Navy would kindly relocate for our charters to go home with lots of fish.

How wonderful would it be if the ship was the *USNS Comfort*? I wondered if the voice of the sailor standing by on the ship-to-ship radio would be one I had heard before. The doctors and nurses onboard would know exactly what to do to check out Eric and me. The best thing of all would be getting picked up by an American vessel. Considering there are so few hospital ships.

As the ship came closer, my excitement and sheer gratitude began to grow exponentially. The form was growing larger, and the shape was becoming more distinct. It seemed almost surreal how Eric and I would be rescued so quickly. The airplane sighting had been a long shot, but there was more hope in one of the passengers on this ship seeing us.

This time the captain and I would need to be more conscientious about deploying the flares so we could provide the vessel the best opportunity to see them. The waves would actually give us a line-of-sight advantage. To strike the handheld flares, we needed to be in the water, which would leave only our heads out of the water. The earth curves eight inches per mile. In flat conditions with our eyes about eight inches above the sea surface, it is about one mile to the horizon. The crest of a five-foot wave would give us an extra two miles of visibility. The crew way up there on the ship would certainly have a height advantage to see us.

Attempting to strike the flares while on the bagged surfboard could really go badly. An ember from the flare might burn a hole in the bag and cause both to slowly smolder away. While trying to strike the flare, I could lose my balance, fall off the side of the board, and go underwater. This was going to be our salvation. I could not mess this up. Lighting the flares from in the water was certainly going to be the best option.

Eric and I continued to watch the ship as it came ever closer. The flares were at the ready to signal. The shape was about to reveal the identity of the type of vessel. Was it commercial? If so, we would want to focus the bulk of our signaling effort while we were head-on to the ship's front quarter. There would likely not be anyone on deck, so we would need to get the attention of the few crew members looking out on the bridge deck. If it was a cruise ship, it would provide the opportunity of having eyes looking forward, to the side, and off the stern.

We could see the shape of the ship's stem and the flare of her bow now. As a ship travels through the waves, the stem is designed to smoothly meet them while the flare of the bow sheds the water and slows the descent of the bow as it drops down into the waves. The funnel or smoke stack appeared to be toward the stern of the white ship. There was a light plume of exhaust rising up and trailing almost horizontally behind the ship. The shape of the plume let us know the ship was making way at a good speed, and the wind above the surface of the sea was blowing at a pretty good clip. Then, the unknown became known. The clarity of recognition was like watching a slide show where the photo switches from an out of focus, blurry shape to a crisp, high-definition image.

"It's a cruise ship!" Eric yelled out.

"There must be thousands of people on there. This time we're going to be rescued!" I said to Captain Eric.

The white ship looked like one from the Carnival Cruise Lines, maybe the *Ecstasy*. Visions of the ship's master and officers in their white uniforms entered my mind, like a scene from the old *Love Boat* television series I used to watch as a kid. The bridge of the ship extended all the way across the front of the ship from the port to starboard side, with its wings extending over the edge of the ship. The bridge had to be close to a hundred feet above the waterline, creating a perfect view of the ocean for the crew. I imagined them standing up there with binoculars scanning the sea out to twelve or thirteen miles. The crew would know exactly what they were looking at when our distress flares and smoke were spotted.

I prayed, "Thank you, Lord, for hearing and answering my prayer. My faith was weak before when the airplane passed us. Forgive me. Surely you have provided our salvation in a wonderful way."

When we were off the starboard front quarter of the ship, I ignited the first flare on the second attempt with a crisp, sharp strike of the igniter. The bright orange smoke erupted out of the end of the tube into a plume flowing downwind. The increased wind speed was not helping our cause, as it kept the smoke low and dispersed it quickly.

A round was loaded into the flare gun and fired in an arc perpendicular to their intended course. I imagined how the bright red ball of fire was catching the eye of officers on watch. I thought of how the Master probably just gave the order, "Maintain a fix on the distress signal position." A seaman worth his salt never takes his eyes off the target until he has an approximate heading and distance. Possibly, the next order was for an inertia stop, which would allow the ship to drift to a stop. Maybe the order was for a crash stop used only in emergency situations when engines are shifted from ahead to full astern. There could have been an order to the helmsman, "Hard to Starboard," for the ship to come around to the right. If the ship was making twenty knots, it could be a couple minutes before there would be a significant change in direction.

I deployed another flare. We were now directly off to the side of the cruise ship at the closest point that we could be for the flares to be most visible to her. The ship must have been six miles or so away. This was going to be our best and only chance. It was time for the grand finale of the fireworks show. Captain Eric and I started creating our big scene with flares. *The cruise ship's sundeck must be well over a hundred feet above the waterline. There is no way anyone looking out from the highest passenger deck could miss us.*

Eric and I had improved our ability to ignite the candle flares. The flares could be activated now within two strikes. The handheld orange smoke flares had a burn time of approximately one minute, whereas the red handheld flares burn time was for three minutes. With each flare, our anticipation of hope grew. I had never been on a cruise ship before, but I did know there was a lot of delicious food we would be feasting on. They would have dry clothes and shoes for our prune-like feet. *There are so many fun things to do on that ship, but I really just want a drink of water and a nap,* I thought.

Cruise ships always a lot more passengers than crew members, so it wouldn't be a big deal if we were unable to get the officer's attention while we were off their front quarter. Someone could be staring out the window of their stateroom, sitting on a private balcony, looking out the window of one of those fancy restaurants or even looking out over the ocean from one of the upper decks. A hundred people must be looking out over the beautiful sea. Someone had to see us down there. After all, the sun was shining and the surfboard bag was so reflective.

Thoughts of a passenger alerting a crew member or notifying a deckhand of the flare seen off to the side of the ship passed through my mind. The deckhand would then report up to the bridge. Any time now, they would spot us in the lenses of their high-powered binoculars. Surely, it would be any moment now.

New hope soared in my heart as the ship's stern quarter neared us because people often like to stand at the stern. The mixed-up water behind the ship from each blade of the propeller grabbed a piece of the sea to push the massive ship forward. The colors are an ever-changing mixture of blues and whites. *Passengers will be there, and they will see us. The helmsman will be altering course any time now,* I thought.

Shockingly, the cruise ship's speed and course never changed. It just continued to grow smaller and smaller until it was out of sight. How was this possible? If only we had one of the smoke canisters to pop... I had seen them so many times as a kid at US Navy Special Forces demonstrations with my neighbor. There seemed to be nothing good coming out of the cruise ship passing us. We had just used up our main supply of signals. Now we had only two remaining bullets for the twelve-gauge pistol. Our lifelines were gone.

The feeling of watching the ship of salvation go over the horizon was so much more crushing than watching the plane fly out of sight. This was our real chance of making it through this ordeal. After it disappeared, not one word was mentioned between Eric and I about the ship beyond our sight. It continued on its way, totally unaware of the mariners' hopes of survival in its wake.

The reality of our situation sank heavily into the core of my soul. Our chance of rescue would not get much better than the opportunity provided by the ship. *Why is it not in*

Your will, God, for Eric and me to be saved? Maybe I am not worthy, but he is. There was no hope for survival left in me. I figured it would only be a matter of time before I was dead.

It was about two o'clock in the afternoon, nine hours since my thirst had been quenched last, and the waves were getting bigger. I had to push those growing seeds of darkness out of my mind. "As long as I'm breathing and not bleeding out, I must find hope," I told myself.

The best way to proceed beyond this latest challenge was to get back to work focusing on what needed to be done to survive. There may be another cruise ship, military ship, or even a Cuban commercial fishing boat out there somewhere. The EPRIB and life raft were out there somewhere too. I had to allow my survival instinct to return to the motivation level experienced prior to the passing of the plane and cruise ship. Honestly, though, it was only a mask for the true feelings I held deep inside. I was going to drown or get ripped apart by the sharks. Watching the cruise ship leaving was crippling.

God is not done with me yet. Only He knows how much I can handle, and the Bible says He will not give us more than we can handle. There had to be a great message He wanted me to learn. What'll be next? Following every struggle, there had been a blessing to keep Captain Eric and me going—and give us hope.

My first flounder fishing trip with Dad on the Eastern Shore of Virginia.

CHAPTER 8:

ROUGH SEAS AND FADING HOPE

The easterly wind was really starting to pick up, the occasional gust of twenty nautical miles per hour were occurring much more frequently. At about four o'clock in the evening, Captain Eric and I finally had the conversation we were both dreading.

"Johnny, if we don't find the EPRIB, we probably are not going to make it out of this. We have to have the EPIRB."

His tone was very serious, and I knew the meaning behind his words. It must have been very hard for him to say these words that were actually an order. If he had the strength, he would have taken on the mission himself. The violent sea had taken too much of his energy away. The unspoken orders from my captain were to go find the EPIRB and activate the signal.

My soul was wrecked thinking about going out on another search for the EPIRB in the terrible sea state that was developing. I knew this time it would be different because it was a one-way trip. The debris line that provided my path on the first excursion to search the line was separating. The

Gulf Stream current and the wind direction were at odds with each other, creating a uniquely choppy sea state of large waves.

"Eric, I don't feel like I covered the diagonal line as thoroughly as I needed to. I just have a gut feeling the EPRIB or life raft could be there," I replied in an effort to shed hope on the task.

I knew when I set out on the search, the likelihood of ever seeing my captain again was slim to none. Maybe Eric knew my whole life was ahead of me and my best opportunity for rescue was to find the EPRIB. I needed to cover as much of the debris as possible before the wind and the waves scattered it across many square miles of sea surface. The final search was the best scenario for my future. I didn't know if this was a plan for the captain to go down with the ship. It was sickening to say what might be my last words to Captain Eric Bingham.

"Okay, Cap. I'm going to find the EPIRB. I want you to know that when I find it and activate the signal, we're not going to stop searching until we find you. I promise." I had to find it because the thought of being a failure again was more than I could bear.

Eric and I then switched places. He gave me the surfboard as he took hold of the engine hatch and bench-seat cushion. I reluctantly climbed up with my chest on the board and kicked the nose around to the down sea direction where the debris line was. With my unspoken orders, I once again started the journey on the path that was once narrow.

I wondered, *How would I explain this to Lisa? I was rescued, but we couldn't find Eric. There would be no way to explain to her the last moments of her husband's life. There would be no closure to give her peace. How would I explain to her that I failed over and over again to obtain the resources we needed to save our lives? I would rather die.* I continued my course paddling away from Eric.

"Dear Lord, please be with us. I trust you with all my heart. Please make my path straight. Protect my mind from wavering."

A small, black, rubber object caught my eye. I struggled for our paths to meet while bobbing up and down on the waves. It was a woman's sandal. I recognized that it belonged to the boss's daughter. For a brief moment, the chaos pulsed as I reflected on our time in Chub Cay, Bahamas. The night was like a scene out of *Captain Ron*. The boss, his wife and daughter, Eric, and I had the rum flowing, the music turned up, and were dancing in the salon of the *Anhinga*. In the middle of a terrifying situation, the reflection brought joy to my heart. I tied her shoe to my life jacket as a token of hope that if I made it out of this situation, I might have the nerve to return it to her.

With my new addition of hope attached, I pressed on searching for the yellow ditch-bag containing the safety gear. Staying on the lookout for the diagonal line was very important because I knew that was the most likely location to find the EPIRB. Finding the life raft would have been nice, but deploying it if found was not an option that would help to save Eric. We were too far away from each other, and the wind would carry the life raft away from him.

The wind speeds and conditions had approached the limits to where we typically cancel our offshore charters for the safety of the passengers and vessel. Although, sometimes during high profile billfish tournaments, we were forced to fish in small craft advisory conditions. The results are typically less fish, possible injuries, and a certainty of bruises and necessary repairs to the boat.

Oftentimes, the charter customers have paid their deposit, traveled from another state, and are extremely excited. With anticipation in their bones, they come to the marina as we back into the slip the evening before their trip in hopes of catching a glimpse of the day's catch. Their anticipation is on high for what they might catch on the outer limits of tomorrow.

One morning, the offshore waters forecast had current windspeed of fifteen to twenty knot winds sustained with gusts to twenty-five knots. Winds were expected to reach twenty-five to thirty knots sustained by midmorning. We call this a "TRAP" because we would arrive to the fishing grounds sixty miles offshore at the same time the wind does. Effectively trolling in such winds is nearly impossible and not safe, so as a fleet, we decided offshore trips were cancelled. In times like those, mates don't even bring the rods out into the cockpit to give the arriving charter the subliminal message, "We aren't going today." Every now and then, the charter effectively begs or there are bills to pay so the engines fire up and rods come out anyway. It only takes one charter boat to leave the slip for everyone else to be almost forced to go.

This particular breezy morning, the customers arrived at a quarter to five for a five o'clock departure. They had tied one on the night before and were still probably a little drunk. They were so excited, they didn't want to hear any part of it not being safe to go out, even though they had the option to reschedule or get a refund of deposit. It had not been a marginal forecast at all. I could sense the frustration growing in Captain Steve's face and voice as a group of six men insisted on going. Mt. Saint Helens had nothing on Steve in that moment as he was about to blow up. The captain's forearms may not have been quite as large as Popeye the Sailor Man's, but you definitely wouldn't want him to get his hands on you.

He told the spokesman of the group as he pointed out to the dark end of the dock, "Look, You and I can go down there to the end of the dock and I can whip your a__ right now, and then I'll wipe up the blood with one of your buddies. Or, I can take you out to fish and break the boat and you. You'll feel the same either way. What do you want to do?"

The "spokesman" was all worried looks and demure voice now. "Is it really going to be that bad out there today, captain?"

"Yes, sir. That is what I've been trying to tell you," Steve replied. Ironically, the name of the boat Steve captained was *No Problem*.

"Okay, captain. We'd like to look at the booking calendar to pick another day to come back."

It was getting rough. Eric and I were now separated in the Gulf Stream. Increased wave height accompanied the increased wind speeds. The wave heights were becoming more consistent six-footers with the space or duration between the tops of the waves getting shorter. Basically, the sea surface conditions were starting to deteriorate as the waves became choppy with the shorter distance between the crests of the waves. The conflicting waves and current made the surface resemble the inside of a washing machine.

I shook at the overwhelming sight of the face of the waves. As a surfer, so often I had welcomed this spectacle knowing that when I felt the lift on the tail of the surfboard followed by the forward thrust of the ocean's power, I'd be racing down the face of an overhead wave. The adrenaline flowing through my veins while surfing a hurricane ground swell in Hatteras, North Carolina, was composed of more excitement than fear. But there was no excitement while lost in the grip of this tempest. The adrenaline racing through my veins was fueled by fear with each advancing wave in the Gulf Stream. I did not have a choice between the fight or flight responses. There was no beach to retreat to for rest from the fury. Most beaches would be closed to swimming in lesser conditions. My only option was to fight.

As I clumsily paddled the surfboard, the broadside wind peppered my face with the salty sea spray. I would tuck down to hide my face with each stroke of my upwind arm. The droplets of salt water were being blown into the side of my face and eyes. The wind was blowing the splash from my left arm slapping the water, along with the water droplets running off my arm. The salt drops of water were like small bee stings as they came into contact with the microscopic lacerations and burns on my face.

My struggle to maintain any control of the surfboard was becoming really difficult. The water was continuing to saturate the surfboard's foam construction, which was starting to affect the board's stability. I wondered if I had doomed my fate by going out to look for the EPIRB again. How much of my stored energy, which was more precious than gold or jewels, had I spent on this failed endeavor?

Having reached what appeared to be the end of the diagonal line, I had nothing to show for all the effort put into finding the critical life safety gear. I was so certain it had to be in this particular line of debris that I had failed to thoroughly cover during the first search. All hope for our survival was in finding at least the EPIRB or the life raft on the venture. I had risked everything on this mission—our lives and my required energy to sustain myself. "God, it's not fair that I sacrificed so much to get nothing in return," I lamented. "Why have You done this to me?"

I was mad at God again. The same God who had allowed the plane to continue to fly past and the cruise ship to go over the horizon. I do not know how many Sundays I heard the preacher say, "God will never leave you or forsake you." It certainly felt like God had left and forsaken me.

There was no other option. I prayed again, "Dear Lord, thank You for the blessing You have provided so far. I am really scared and need to know You are with me. I hope Your will is for me to see Blackwater Baptist again. If You allow it to happen, I'll try to listen to the preacher more and daydream less about fish in the lake painted in the mural behind him."

Blackwater Baptist Church was founded in 1774. Located in the rural southern end of Virginia Beach, four generations of the Savage family have called this church "home."

I was having a hard time seeing any blessings because of my anger toward God. Praying helped change my attitude for a little while. It also made it easier to reflect on all He had provided. There were things to be thankful for. *Eric and I were allowed to escape the* Anhinga *without entrapment as she went down. Milt and Neal were not on the boat. We were surrounded by an awesome creation. We were provided with necessary resources from amidst the debris. I was still alive.* These thoughts of praise quickly disappeared as I let the Devil fill my mind with darkness, though.

I was at the end of the diagonal debris line, and the negative thoughts were on the rise as a result of my failure. Eric was floating somewhere out there far from my sight. I thought maybe by some slight chance I had missed the EPIRB or life raft somewhere on the other line that went down sea. If only I could find the debris, maybe I could get back to Eric. At the time, I knew in my heart the probability of finding Eric again was pretty much impossible. Another foothold in the death of hope.

It was time to return to the mission. Once again, I had to stop the evolving thoughts of darkness. I was able to find the main down sea debris line by paddling through the trough on the first expedition in search of the EPRIB. I would do the same. The seas were getting more confusing as the wind and current were at opposing angles to each other. The true direction I needed to paddle to remain in the primary trough was going to be a challenge to maintain. The overall attempt would be much more difficult than it was the last time, with a greater risk of becoming lost. Although, I was already lost. The waves were larger, and the whitecaps were more prevalent.

The term "going through the trough" is not a term of remaining in the lower trough portion of the wave. It's a term used when we troll in a direction that runs more or less parallel to the length of the wave. This maneuver puts the vessel at the greatest risk of capsizing because the vessel's length or broadside is toward the face of the wave. Vessels from rowboats to supercarrier are extremely vulnerable when the wave is traveling on the perpendicular side of the vessel and strikes it on the side.

In addition to the challenges of being uncertain which way I should go, there was no escaping the chills. Hypothermia was progressing. I knew the symptoms would worsen in the near future.

I started paddling through what appeared to be the trough. I was so exhausted from the fight to stay alive and the mental anguish of knowing I had failed my captain. It required so much effort each time I lifted and reached my arm to grab a handful of water to propel myself forward. My muscles were contracting and extending in a sluggish unison just trying to keep my body parts on the surfboard. Body parts in the water were at risk because predators prey on the weak. I thought about the unknown lurking below. *Was it even worth it to exert so much energy just to remain on the surfboard and bag?* The exterior of the bag was somewhat slippery. It lacked the specially formulated tropical wax that was on the surfboard inside of the bag. Surf wax is rubbed on the top of surfboard to provide a tacky surface for a surfer's' feet to grip the board, allowing twisting and turning maneuvers.

I desperately tried to make paddling the only reason any body part was in the water, but the sea conditions were not helping. As the waves came against my broadside, I had to extend an arm, leg, or both to the high side in an attempt to counterbalance. I felt like a tightrope walker out of his element. Unfortunately, there were many times this did not work. Off the side I would go, clinging to the board and capsizing into the sea. Fortunately, I was usually able to inhale gasps of air just before rolling over.

Periodically, the tops of the waves would lose their structure as the crest of the wave traveled faster than the trough section below it, causing the top to forcefully crumble over and create a whitecap. There were a couple times I was unexpectedly struck on the side by one. The whitecaps were like defensive ends in football, hitting me from the side and knocking me off the board before I had a chance to gasp a breath of air.

I had cleared the scattered debris of the diagonal line. It had been a while since there was evidence of the disaster floating around me. Regardless of the sea surface conditions, I had to keep pushing on through the trough and dealing with the occasional requirement for a burst of energy to right myself and scramble back atop the bagged surfboard. *Just one more stroke*, and then another, as trough and crest passed beneath the board. I envied them as I thought about how they would eventually strike shore many miles away. As the crest of waves passed, the wind pelted my face with sprays of water even worse than the droplets coming off my arm.

After either an eternity or twenty minutes, I started to see debris again. Unfortunately, it was everywhere and without form—a total scattered mess of wood, foam, and plastics. I realized I was now truly lost. The waves appeared to be coming from two different directions. This is possible when a distant low-pressure system sends a ground swell in one direction with wind-driven waves coming from another. The sea conditions had certainly become worse. Like a child who just lost their mother in a superstore, uncertainty gripped me. I wrapped myself around the surfboard with no idea of what to do.

I had failed to find the EPRIB and was now lost. The feeling of being worthless was crushing and controlling my mind. Eric and I were both going to die because I was unable to execute the mission of finding the beacon or life raft.

I had to report my failure to Captain Eric, but it was going to be impossible to find him. The thoughts of certain death and darkness returned to torment me. *You are a failure. You're going to die out here alone. One simple task and you couldn't execute it. You're going to drown or maybe you'll be ripped to shreds by the sharks when the sun goes down. You know that's when they feed. You will never see them coming in the dark. You can't possibly hang on that long, can you?*

To escape the darkness overcoming my mind, I righted myself on the surfboard and started to dig in once more in a direction that seemed like up-sea. This time, it was different. I had no confidence in the direction I was paddling. It was such a struggle. Fighting to make any headway in the seven-foot seas was an exhausting struggle. The surfboard had become so waterlogged, it was nearly impossible to manage. If only the waves that were charging toward me were coming from one direction, I could angle diagonally up the face to make headway in a zigzag pattern.

As I scanned the horizon, my eyes would lock on any similar wreckage I could find to put the puzzle back together. Just as the wind, waves, and currents had formed the lines of the *Anhinga*'s debris, the increased wind and waves were overpowering the current, causing the definitive lines to be totally nonexistent now. The debris was scattering, and now with sky thick with storm clouds, it was even harder to see the wreckage.

I was no doubt lost. I was certain, without any speck of hope at all, I would never see my captain again. *I am giving up. I can't do it.* The Type II life jacket I was wearing was made for a pond, lake, or some other inland body of water. When I was a kid, Dad bought me the same kind of life jacket for the creeks and swamps of Blackwater. The Type II was unable to withstand the open high seas and was already ripping apart. *I will surely die.*

The thought of hypothermia was returning. My shivering was becoming more pronounced. I thought about how hypothermia progresses to immobilize its victims. When the life jacket ripped all the way apart, I may not be able to swim. My body would drift down into the deep, unable to kick back up for a gasp of air. Remembering the water temperature was in the upper seventies, I thought, *There's no way this could be hypothermia.* But it was the beginning stages. *Hey dummy, think about what you went to school for. Your core temperature is dropping, and there is nothing you can do about it. Your body is being saturated in water that is probably twenty degrees lower than your body temperature.*

More and more, dying was becoming the only way to free myself from the pain, struggle, loneliness, and total failure. The devil had planted seeds in my mind of the only two possible outcomes. These seeds were growing very quickly now. Jack's beanstalk beans had nothing on how fast these dark thoughts were growing. I was going to drown or get eaten by sharks.

Right or wrong, I rationalized my choice. I was not going to endure the pain of being eaten by the sharks. I would simply take my failing life jacket off and then roll off the surfboard into the deep beautiful blue sea. As my body went under, I would exhale the air out of my lungs at the point where my body started to feel buoyant. With my legs together and arms reaching toward heaven I would sink like a straight rod heading toward the abyss. Once I got down to twenty or thirty feet, I would force myself down deeper. I knew without fins on my feet, I would not have the strength to return to the surface even if I tried.

When my body could no longer restrain its desire for life-sustaining oxygen, the involuntary reflex might attempt to bring air into my lungs. As the water filled my lungs, it would probably be extremely painful, but not as painful as sharks pulling off my limbs. The convulsions might come as my body responded to the invading seawater. Or, maybe I would simply pass out due to lack of oxygen as my body sunk. In any case, I would soon find out for certain whether Jesus really died to forgive my sins.

CHAPTER 9

RELEASE ME FROM THE CHAOS

My thoughts then returned to my family and friends back home in Virginia. *I wished there was some way to give my parents the assurance that I was at peace and rest. I would be fortunate enough to die in my favorite place, in the Bluewater.* I had such a desire to say, "I love you," "Please don't be hurt," and "Goodbye." They had always been so supportive of my choice to fish. So many times, had they been on the dock in Rudee Inlet waiting for us to back into the slip. *They will miss it.*

My sister, Shari, and her husband, Darren, would have been very hurt too. I thought, *I'd like to thank him for taking this bratty little kid along on their beach dates and introducing me to surfing. It was so wonderful to be at their house for Christmas and see my nephew for the first and only time. I hope Shari and Darren get that old twin fin Wave Riding Vehicle surfboard that he fixed and gave to me. Maybe they could find somewhere to store my metallic royal blue and white Bronco for Michael to drive in sixteen years.*

Aunt Donna and Uncle Joe will have had a hard time with it too. We have had so much fun together this winter working on projects around the house. I hope she'll remember the joy we had spending time together after so many years of being separated by distance. Our blood and love for each other had bound us together. It was priceless to be able to spend so much time together with my cousins, Joey and Torey. Joey didn't even get mad at me for trying to pee in his closet after a night of partying in downtown West Palm Beach. Torey has such a kind heart. This is going to hurt her so deeply.

I wanted to give Cousin Joey the watch on my wrist. The face was covered in what looked like sandpaper from the fine to course grit that had scratched the crystal in every direction. *Each of these scars are the unique signature from all of the marlins' bills that have wielded their instrument of battle against my wrist as they were being released.*

I had no written will for my parents to know how to distribute my belongings. *What all had I left in my bedroom closet when I headed to Palm Beach?* Mike would have had to clean up and pack my stuff. He was not only a roommate; he was like the brother I never had. *It will be hard for him.* My very first shotgun was a Remington, model 1100, twenty gauge with a blue barrel and beautiful varnished shock. It was in the closet at the condo. I wanted for Mike to keep it to remember all the great times we had together.

Mike and I holding the sailfish he caught in 1997 while we were moving the boat from Puerto Aventuras to Cancún. Captain Sean was at the helm of *Release Me*, a fifty-eight-foot Viking Yacht.

There was so much fishing tackle at my parents'. I hoped it would go to my buddies in remembrance of all the wild and crazy times we had together. Never again would I pack into the cab of a farm tractor at two o'clock in the morning with Billy or Neal and try to sneak out of the barn and move past the house to pull one of our buried trucks out of the bean field. *If only Jason and Joey can each have a fishing rod to remember all of the nights we closed down the bars at the beach.* Thoughts of the night the snow was deep enough at the Virginia Beach Oceanfront for us to kick the fins off a surfboard, tie a ski rope to the back of Pat's truck, and surf down Atlantic Avenue flashed through my head. *How did we not go to jail?* I wanted Jay to have a rod, too, so he could remember all of the contagious laughs we had together. He couldn't catch enough air to speak while the tears were flowing from his eyes. One of us always had to stop laughing so we didn't pass out from not breathing. I hoped his wife, Caroline, would forgive me for telling her what's in a hot dog.

I wanted Brian to have a rod too. I felt so bad for all of those tore-out-of-the-frame nights at the Virginia Beach Oceanfront bars where we were able to sneak him in the back door. Fresh from the Virginia Tech frats, he would pound every shot we gave him until he got so drunk he could hardly stand. Brian would get dropped off on the deck of the *Miss Behaven* a couple hours before the charter showed up. Around 8:30 p.m., I would hear chattering on the radio. It was Brian's captain venting to my captain. Sure enough, as soon as their conversation ended, Captain Dave would lean over the rail.

"Hey, Johnny. Joe is on the radio fussing about Brian being worthless today. What did you do to him last night?"

I looked up to the bridge and replied, "Well, Cap, I recon if you're dumb, you better be tough. We're breaking him in."

Captain Dave would graciously smile and shake his head as if he were remembering his younger days as a mate.

I felt terrible. I had committed to working for Captain Steve on the *Chaos*, a brand-new fifty-foot Viking Yacht that we were going to run charters on for Bill and "Rockin' Rod". I was going to miss out on fishing all the mid-Atlantic, big money, marlin fishing tournaments, but mostly I would miss the chance to catch a one-thousand pounder in Bermuda.

I was so looking forward to spending a couple of weeks at the Bluewater Yacht Sales service yard as they finished rigging out the Chaos for us to make the Big Rock Blue Marlin and the Hatteras Marlin Club tournaments. Captain Steve was known for being one of the best. *I could have learned so much more from him. I hate that I'm going to die out here and leave Steve looking for a new mate.*

The comradery in the boat yard was one of work and play. There would be no cold beers on Bayne's boat at the end of the day. There would be no lessons about the state-of-the-art Viking systems from Craig, the yard manager. Earle, one of the owners of Bluewater, was always so generous with T-shirts that had a new design every year. Although I had never worked on a yacht purchased from his brokerage, he was always so kind to me. I would have liked to get to know him better.

I know that Captain Dave is not happy with me right now. If only we could have parted ways on better terms. He'd taught me so much about fishing and maintaining and handling a boat. I felt bad. We had been a team for five years, and a deep relationship had developed with the regular charter customers. *I have deep regret, and that is no way to die.*

Captain Dave's boat has a very fitting name—*High Hopes*—and it was the nicest charter boat in Rudee Inlet. It was a blessing to work for him. If it were not for Captain Dave, I might not have been praying so much for the Lord to save us. I loved to lay there on the front bench and listen to him each morning when he prayed for the fleet as the sun was just starting to show its glow in the east. I wondered how many people had accepted the love and forgiveness of Jesus through Captain Dave. *I hope he'll forgive me. I wish I could have told him goodbye and I'm sorry.*

I really did not want to die, but it was the only way out. People who commit suicide are making a choice to end their life and leave their loved ones behind to grieve the pain of a life wasted. No one would ever know I made a choice to rob them by ending the struggle myself. *Everyone knows we cannot live long in the water, so they'll think I died as others lost at sea. They will never know I made the better choice, to drown.*

The boss's daughter would never get the shoe tied to my life jacket. It would be the only personal effect we could give the boss from his beautiful boat. *He will never know what happened to his boat. He is such a good man, and he doesn't deserve to go through the rest of his life wondering about the last moments of his crew. All because I failed to find the EPIRB.*

I looked to the sky and said,

"Dear Lord, thank you for the many blessings you have given to me. Thank you for saving me that night on the Pungo Ferry Bridge when the truck flipped over. I did not deserve to be saved then. Thank you for my family and friends. Please comfort them. Thank you for bringing my family to Blackwater Baptist Church and the loving people of the community. Thank you for Jesus going to the cross to shed his blood to forgive my many sins. Lord, please do not see this suicide as sin. I feel like I don't have any other choice. Please forgive me. In Jesus's name, amen."

The final task in preparing to die had been completed. It was time to end my life. I sat up on the surfboard with my legs clinging tightly. The insufficient life jacket had a single strap that went around the chest to snap into a plastic buckle. It was the only way the jacket was secured to the user. There was not even a pair of cloth ribbons at the neck to secure the head from sliding out of the device should the chest strap be too loose or come unfastened.

The sky was cloudy as I shifted my slightly shivering body on the surfboard like a professional bull rider striving to reach eight seconds. I took in one last view of the beautiful blue water. I was finished—time to roll under and end the living nightmare. The free end of the strap was situated so it wouldn't tangle. With my right hand, I reached up to the plastic clasp with my index finger and thumb on each of the release buttons and squeezed. The male side of the buckle was free, and the pressure of the strap around my chest faded as the free end of the buckle was pulled away and let go.

I was confident in my decision. With a hand on each of the floatation sides of the life jacket, I pulled them apart and lifted it up and over my head. I was free of the final barrier. There would be no more failures. The waves were approaching from the right. My cold and exhausted body started to lean as the crest of a wave passed beneath. I was actually ending my life. I would soon know if God is real.

CHAPTER 10:

DIVINE INTERVENTION

"Do not fear, for I have redeemed you. I have summoned you by name; you are mine. When you pass through the waters, I will be with you."

ISAIAH 43: 1-2 NIV

While in the process of rolling under to end it all, an amazing feeling of warmth and strength overcame my entire body. An instinctual feeling that the sensation I was experiencing was not of the world took hold of me. At the very least, I knew this burst of strength could not have come from myself. I frantically stopped my descent by locking my legs around the surfboard and grabbing the life jacket before it drifted out of reach.

I repositioned my body on the surfboard. I didn't fully understand what had just happened to my body. God showed up in a big way. What happened next was awesome.

Sitting up with renewed strength and the board positioned just as it was prior to rolling off, I heard an audible voice! I turned in the direction I'd heard the instruction coming from. It came from off and behind my right shoulder, but there was no one there.

There couldn't possibly have been anyone there. I was somewhere in the middle of the sea between the Florida Keys, Cuba, and the Bahamas, for goodness' sake. But there was no doubt I'd heard a voice come into my ears. I was amazed I could hear a voice with a tone so comforting in the midst of an angry, roaring sea. It calmly overpowered the wind and the waves of the Gulf Stream with a simple instruction.

"John, you have spent a lot of time out here. Pick your line and paddle it," the heavenly voice proclaimed.

In that very moment, I knew without a doubt God was real and He had never left me. We were going to make it. The line was chosen, and my faith was full.

Whose voice did I hear? It certainly was not Captain Eric, and there was no one else out there. Was it the Holy Spirit? He has only spoken to my inner spirit, never an audible voice to my ears. Was it God or Jesus? Maybe it was an angel or maybe even an archangel. I do not know, but I will one day when I hear the voice again that was able to overpower the sea.

I was amazed at the miraculous event that had just occurred. My symptoms of hypothermia did not line up with physical symptoms that occur when the core temperature drops to ninety-five degrees. Physical Hazards was a course I was required to take in order to graduate from Old Dominion University. The class required safety students to understand the effects of heat and cold on the human body. My dexterity was solid, and my shivering wasn't totally uncontrollable. What I had just heard couldn't be chocked up to being a hallucination.

As the body gets colder and colder, the blood vessels in the extremities begin to constrict to conserve heat in the core of the body with warmer blood. Once the body reaches a certain point, it knows its attempts at survival are futile. The vessels in the extremities open back up, which allows blood to create a warm sensation throughout the body. While I had experienced a warm feeling, it would have been inaccurate to equate it with this process of vessels opening because of the dexterity I still retained just prior to the event. My motor skills were still too fine-tuned at this point to be passed off as a mental condition associated with hypothermia or the ingestion of salt water. I was at the point where saltwater had been sloshing around inside my mouth, but I hadn't ingested that much.

It was time to get back to work. This new inspiration, knowing Eric and I just had to hang on and keep up the fight until rescuers arrived to save us, spurred me forward. The rejoicing and praise in my heart was effusive, although the form in which rescue would come was unknown.

I scanned the horizon in the up-sea direction as I reflected on the command given to me. "Pick your line and paddle it." Picking my line was meant in relation to the directional heading. "Paddle it" was a command to get moving. I watched and watched the waves until, somehow, beyond the capability of my navigation, I was able to find a repeatable pattern. I now had a constant source to provide me direction.

I paddled up steep faces of waves and then glided down their backsides. One after another, they seemed so monstrous. As the board crested the top, the nose of the surf would fall with gravity for a brief second as the board transitioned to the back side of the wave, sort of like a teeter-totter at a playground. Each stroke and each wave passed was one bit closer to Eric and me coming home. I could not trust my eyes. Everything I saw said I was surely going to die, but I knew by faith we would be saved.

If I could take even a mustard seed-sized portion of the faith I held within me at that time and transfer it to someone else, it would be sufficient to save any person contemplating suicide as they go through their darkest hour.

As each wave crested, I took the opportunity to intensify my scan of the sea surface. The crest of the wave had the best vantage point. I had a renewed hope in my soul that the EPIRB or life raft might be found. The debris was extremely scattered and with no form, but maybe, just maybe, I'd pass by the EPIRB. Maybe that was God's plan for our rescue.

I strained to spot the white rectangular engine hatch Captain Eric was hanging onto when I had left. The hatch was still the largest single piece of the *Anhinga* I had come across. He could have been in any direction by then, but the Lord allowed me to see a path through the confused sea. After paddling the course for about forty minutes, I spotted something large. It was rectangular and whitish in color slightly off to my right at about three hundred yards out. I had a target, but the target did not have Eric clinging to it. As the distance was cut to 150 yards, I could tell it was larger than the engine hatch.

I quickly caught a glimpse of another white object. It was beyond and to the left of the large floating rectangle. I could only see it for a brief second, and then it was gone as the waves would rise and fall. This was a common occurrence in these worsening sea conditions. There was a five- to ten-minute gap before I could catch another sighting of some of the floating debris. Reacquiring the location of an object was a challenge. It had to line up perfectly within the sequence of waves. The white object to the left seemed to be playing a game of hide-and-seek with me. I was certain I had spotted something over there, but didn't know when I would see the other object again.

As a sportfishing boat captain, there are two priorities you have for any day out on the water. The first is to safely get everyone back home at the end of the day. The second is to find and catch fish. There have been days when the second priority was achieved because of a single piece of trash floating in the ocean. The rougher it is, the harder it is to maintain visual contact with floating debris to which the fish are attracted. From the elevated position on the flybridge, once the captain has spotted something floating that might be holding a school of fish, the craziest game of hide-and-seek starts. He would often take immediate note of the sun's position and the wave direction to use it to their advantage in finding the floating object that is holding fish. If the captain can maneuver the boat to keep the sun to his back, it is easier to maintain visual contact with the target.

Now, as I bobbed like a piece of flotsam in the Gulf, I maintained the course and focus toward the larger floating object. It started to appear like the large rectangle was flexible, flowing, and forming with the passing waves. It seemed to have depth to it. I wondered if the object was worth expending the energy required to get over to it. The object was large enough for two people to fit on top of it. As I approached at about fifty yards, I recognized what it was and where it had come from. I was overcome with the deepest gratitude when I realized the gift of security that had just been provided.

The gift was an affirmation of how the *Anhinga* must have come apart with her bow deck peeling off or her back breaking. The keel section of a boat is like her spine. The white rectangle flowing with the waves had been in the master stateroom. The boss's stateroom was immediately to the starboard down-below in the living quarters of the *Anhinga*. The master stateroom mattress was directly below the spot where I had seen the crack running across the bow-deck when we hit the bottom of the rogue wave. The queen size mattress would have never made it out if the bow deck and house were still intact with the hull.

The mattress was not as great of a find as I had hoped, but it was still a blessing. It was made of foam, which is why I was able to see it flexing and flowing with the waves. Eric and I were in desperate need of something to get our bodies out of the seawater, which had been sucking the heat and life out of us since morning. This was another case where I was able to look at debris from the *Anhinga* and instantly determine if it could potentially save my life.

The stateroom mattress was certainly determined to be useful. The mattress was not buoyant enough to elevate our bodies out of the water at all, but it would most certainly be able to provide us protection as long as we could stay on top of it. Sunset was not too far off, and that's when the sharks like to feed. I thought, *When I find Eric, we can both get on top of this so none of our body parts are hanging down in the water for a shark to snack on.*

I could not wait to tell Eric what I had found. The question was, which way should I go? The engine hatch and my captain should have been about forty-five degrees from my current position. The ability to return to a particular reference point in the ocean can be very challenging without a compass or some sort of navigation electronics. A fisherman develops an almost instinctive trait after years and years of being on the ocean. The question of which way to go is constantly on a captain's mind while fishing.

Questions raced through my mind as I thought about the best options associated with this latest dilemma. *Find Eric and then come back for the mattress or take the mattress to him? If I left the mattress, would I ever find it again?* I had a strange confidence I would find Eric. This confidence rested in the directional line I was commanded to distinguish in the presence of a confusing wave pattern.

I scanned the ever-changing elevation of the horizon in the direction I sensed the other white object to be. There is a unique characteristic about how boldly the various hues of white stand out on the sea with an overcast sky. The surface of the pelagic waters was littered with whitecaps crumbling over formlessly as the waves proceeded on their journey.

I caught a glimpse of the other white object with a rectangular form. It appeared to be the engine access hatch. My eyes had locked in on the direction of the white form with the intensity of a Tomahawk missile. As our two waves rose in unison, I had absolute confirmation it was the engine hatch and that Captain Eric was still alive and hanging onto it. The master stateroom mattress was within one hundred yards of the captain. This was another gift provided—another little miracle. The heart within my strengthened body was overcome with so much joy and gratitude.

Captain Eric seemed to be equally excited and relieved at our reunion. I noticed he was clinging to something blue that was partially looped around his arm. I thought I recognized the object by its color, but I couldn't be certain.

There always seemed to be a monster to overcome. *How was I going to get this submerged, water-filled structureless mass over to Eric?* If I tried to get behind it and push, it would fold around like a taco shell. If I tried to pull it by grabbing onto the front edge, I would probably end up with a handful of foam as the edge tore off. Pulling it would be the best option. I went back a couple feet from the center of the end closest to Captain Eric and dug my hand through the eight-inch-thick mattress. I was surprised how easily this was accomplished.

With my left arm stretched across the surfboard and my right arm hooked through the newly formed towing hole, I began to act as a human tug boat in the middle of the Gulf of Mexico. With my left arm naturally hanging onto the surfboard for buoyancy, I planned to drag the mattress by using my legs to kick toward Eric's position. The performance would be far from the perfectly streamlined approach of an Olympic swimmer. Nevertheless, I was so thankful for all of those American Red Cross swimming lessons my mother demanded I complete at such an early age.

I had to determine the most efficient and effective stroke to use when making my way across a hundred yards in towering waves. First, I tried the regular fluttering type of kick used with a freestyle or crawl stroke. It seemed to use too much of my energy. Then I tried the jack-knifed scissor-like kick of the sidestroke. It was much easier than the fluttering of the previous attempt. Lastly, I tried the frog-style kick used in the breaststroke. It did not take long to figure out that wasn't going to work. So, it was back to the sidestroke kick to get all the way over to Captain Eric.

This reunion with Eric was very different from when I returned from the first search for the EPIRB and life raft. On the first endeavor, I failed to find things critical to our survival and burned up much of my life-sustaining stored energy in the process. The second endeavor was not a failure. What appeared to be a total loss and waste of time would actually be the greatest moment I had ever experienced in my life. It was without a doubt supernatural. I had found something not of this world that was far more valuable to our survival than the EPRIB or life raft, even though I didn't fully understand it at the time. I'd found hope and a mattress to sustain us until help arrived.

What was I going to tell Eric? He knew the Lord's Prayer, but would he believe what had happened? Would anyone believe what happened? It didn't matter because I knew, without a doubt, I was told to pick a line and paddle. Doing so brought me back to Eric. I wanted to tell him, but I couldn't do it.

As I approached Eric, I let go of the surfboard and swam to him. Even with the noticeable symptoms of hypothermia, the captain maintained his gracious composure.

I told Eric, "I'm sorry, I couldn't find the EPIRB or life raft again. This time, I was able to cover the diagonal line better than before, but they weren't there."

That is when I recognized the blue object Captain Eric was clinging onto. It was my backpack. Eric quickly picked up on my expression as my eyes locked on the little blue double-pocket bag with two dark blue straps.

Eric exclaimed, "It just came floating up to me, so I grabbed it."

"Eric, have you looked inside?"

"Well, no," he replied. Of course he would never do such a thing as violate someone's privacy. It would be like looking in a woman's purse.

With a vocal leap of joy, I announced, "Eric, there are wetsuits in that backpack!"

It astounded us we were provided the perfect gift at the perfect time.

Our reunion gave us incredible hope. We'd wondered for so long if the other was even still alive. Both of us never expected to see each other again when I left to look for the EPIRB. It was a risk we had to take. Like long lost brothers who had not seen each other in decades, we grinned at each other. It was good our souls were filled with so much joy because shadows were getting longer as the sun was on its retreat behind the earth. It felt like the center of the storm was getting close. The wind was increasing steadily, and the waves were getting bigger. Were we about to be in the heart of the storm at feeding time?

Captain Fred Feller (second from right) and my grandfather (far right) holding a white marlin caught onboard the *Gannet*. As a boy, I used to stare at this picture on the wall in my grandfather's garage. It inspired my desire to catch big fish. Fred Feller was the first captain I worked for.

CHAPTER 11:

DESPERADO TO BE SAVED

I had no doubt this was one of those little miracles provided at the right time. Some of the items in the backpack were surfboard leashes; tropical surfboard wax; wax combs; thin, Lycra, long sleeve and short sleeve tops; a "P2" top; and a two millimeter "shorty" wetsuit. Captain Eric's hypothermia was more advanced, so he desperately needed to protect his core temperature. The "P2" was a long sleeve, tight-fitting top that was constructed of a soft cloth material and neoprene. This top was my favorite to tame the chill on days when my upper body temperature needed to be maintained. The compression of the top helped to hold the body heated water close to my skin.

I opened the bag and fished through the contents in search of the "P2" top. I knew it as soon as my hand touched the felt-like material. I handed it to the captain. Eric released the hatch and cushion so he could loosen his life jacket in preparation to squeeze into the compression garment. He shifted his life jacket to the opposite arm as he dressed himself in the rising and falling of the waves. The top fit him nicely. He then rested his chest across the surfboard to get his core closer to the surface of the water.

I took off the ripped life jacket in preparation to put on the Billabong "shorty" wetsuit, which closely resembled the uniform a high school wrestler might wear. I took a deep breath and went under to step each leg into the shorts part of the suit. I came up with a gasp, putting each hand through the large arm holes, and pulled the cord attached to the zipper to close up the back. It helped to keep my stomach and hip area warm, although occasionally a gap would allow the body heated water to flush out.

After putting the life jacket back on, I looked over toward Eric. This was a peaceful moment, because he looked comfortable. Or, at least as comfortable as anyone could be in these harsh conditions. I wondered if I should go ahead and tell him about what had happened with my supernatural encounter. I wanted to tell him God had not left us out here alone. *What if we both don't make it out of this alive?* I didn't understand why it happened, so I decided not to say anything about trying to kill myself and the amazing miracle.

"Eric, there are two surfboard leashes still in the backpack," I said.

"That is wonderful. Let's use them to leash ourselves together," he replied.

"Yes, sir." Each of the leashes consisted of a seven-foot, shock-absorbing, rubber cord with an adjustable neoprene and Velcro collar at one end and two-inch wide nylon fabric loop on the other end. I connected the two nylon-loop-ends together using the eight-inch string designed for tethering the leash to the tail of the surfboard. Then I strapped the one end to my wrist and tossed the other to Eric.

"Here's your end, Cap. Just pull the tab apart and wrap it back around your wrist."

I laid back in the water with my left arm pushed through the hole in the mattress, right arm stretched across the ridged hatch, and the bridge cushion locked between my legs. The front was definitely passing through because the sky was filled with dense clouds with only an occasional break of sun. The beauty of the sunshine with rays beaming to the surface of the ocean outweighed the fear of the sun's evolving march toward the horizon. Wind speed was a steady twenty nautical miles per hour, and the waves were a solid seven to eight feet high. Eric and I stood watch for each other in an attempt to avoid being wrapped up by a Portuguese man-of-war or being blindsided by a breaking whitecap.

I tried to determine which of the two was worse. The sting of the jellyfish creature is extremely painful if there are several stings at one time. I figured getting tackled by the whitecap was the worst.

The whitecaps did not seem so powerful when out fishing among them, but being in the water was a different story. Sometimes Eric and I could hear them before they struck us. The rumbling sound of the water falling over itself gave us time take a deep breath and hold it.

I think the silent ones seemed more terrifying because there wasn't enough time to fill our lungs with air. I would feel a forceful blow to my back as the froth of water sent my body and the flotsam I was holding onto in different directions. The worst was when one of the eight-foot plus monsters would strike and send my body tumbling underwater toward the depths in a display that overpowered the buoyancy of the failing life jacket. As my body tumbled and turned underwater, I would lose my sense of direction to the point where I didn't know which way the surface was. The depth was about six thousand feet where we were. There was no bottom for our feet to push off of to spring us up to the surface like when tumbled by a wave at the beach.

I would have to wait for the forces to subside and the buoyancy of the life jacket to gradually disclose the direction to the surface. Then I would surface with a gasp in an attempt to fill my lungs with the oxygen the wave did not grant before striking. There was a fourteen-foot shock absorber between Eric and I. It was like an umbilical cord between us, stretching our arms, sharing the turmoil inflicted upon the other by the untamed white beast.

The waves and the wind caused me to reflect. I have always been amazed by how fish could so precisely launch an attack on their meal in rough sea conditions. A couple months prior, Little Jimmy had taught the crew a new trick to take advantage of the wind and waves, a way to trick sailfish into thinking the bait was a flying fish. Keith and Bones were other mates on the dock at Sailfish Marina who taught me the fine art of cutting strip baits out of the belly of an Atlantic Bonito. The belly portion of the fillet would be trimmed down to just the shiny skin with about an eighth of an inch of meat underneath. The individual baits would be cut out to about one inch wide by nine inches long, then trimmed to a taper at each end.

The bait had to be perfectly connected to the hook in order to pull through the water and fly as it popped out of the wave. The strip was measured for the hook to penetrate the meat and skin, allowing the leading edge of the strip to be tied to the eye of the hook. The front of the flying fish look-a-like was then dressed up with a skirt-like covering called a sea witch.

This sea witch was made of eight-inch nylon hair wrapped around and secured to a quarter ounce lead head. The head of the sea witch had a hole for the fishing line to pass through, allowing it to rest on the eye of the hook.

The first time I put one of these on a long rigger on a rough day, I could not believe what my eyes were seeing. When trolling, the bait came out of the top of the wave just right for the wind to catch the fish line suspended in the air and caused the strip bait to fly like an actual flying fish. Many times, a sailfish, mackerel, or even a shark had jumped out of the same wave flying behind the bait. Then, like a football receiver going long, the fish's open mouth would land on the bait. "Fish-On!"

I wondered what we must look like from below. Could a shark launch and land on us with an open mouth the same way as the fish had on our flying fish bait? I realized I was falling back into the trap of doubt. I quickly had to cast out the dark thought, which was a contradiction to knowing by faith we would be saved. Those thoughts had to be captured before they could develop.

Reflecting on my captain and friends taking the time to teach me new techniques was peaceful. In a desire for additional calmness, I thought about some of my other friends who were mates on the Sailfish Marina Charter Dock. I wondered where Jimbo, Bootsy, Scotty, and the Fields brothers were fishing. We were all like a brotherhood that formed, because most of us had come together for the sailfish season in Palm Beach from places like Montauk, Cape May, Ocean City, Virginia Beach, the Outer Banks of North Carolina, and Charleston. The mates Fraternity House for the season was located in Jupiter, Florida, where there was a stack of mattresses in one room that went to the ceiling. I found myself laughing at thoughts of the Jupiter House craziness with Munford, Rob, and the crew.

The laughter took my mind off of the plywood engine hatch that was barely buoyant enough to float itself, much less a one-hundred-ninety-pound survivor. I was certainly grateful for the pain it caused while trying to hang onto the thing rather than not having any pain as my corpse drifted to the bottom.

If I wasn't holding onto it tight enough, my fingers would slip as a whitecap broke, snatching on the flat, solid surface. It had become agonizing as the hard edge of the plywood pressed into the side of my rib cage and my right-hand fingers curled around the far edge of the plywood to pull it in toward my body in an attempt to gain control and contact with the hatch. I had been clinching the plywood for so long the pain in my fingers reminded me of a game we used to play on the school bus.

The rides from the swamps of Blackwater to town were very long. My parents' house was the earliest bus stop in the whole city of Virginia Beach. I don't recall what we called this game, but we would curl our fingers over and hook our hands. Then, with fingers hooked into each other, we'd pull back as hard as we could for about a minute. Next, our hands would unhook, but your own fingers would remain locked in curl. The point of the game was to experience the pain of the player's fingers opening. It was a dumb game.

I needed some brief relief from the pain of being locked onto the hatch for so long. I hoped I could also reposition to new pressure points against my body. There didn't seem to be a risk of the hatch drifting beyond my ability to regain it, so I let go. The relief from the pressure digging into my side was amazing. When I tried to open my curled fingers, the pain pierced through the knuckles of my right hand as if each finger was being detached at the joint. How foolish I'd been to seek this pain in my younger days.

Within a few minutes, the pain in my fingers was gone, just as it had back on the school bus. It felt freeing to be able to tread water without trying to hang on to the hatch. The peace of the moment was calming to the soul. I had learned to cherish those rare opportunities as they were given to Eric and me. The moments of peace were like a gift from above.

This moment of peace was short-lived as, all of a sudden, I felt the band of my scarred Citizens watch release from my left wrist as I was treading water. With my feet scissor kicking and my arms out diagonally swaying forward and back, I felt something unexpectedly touch the palm of my hand in mid-stroke. I wanted to jerk back due to the uncertainty on what had touched my hand, but I grasped the object in my hand anyway. It was the watch.

I didn't really understand how the watch band could have failed. The watch had recently been to the jeweler to replace the pins connecting the band to the watch, so how did this happen? Maybe the pins bent during the impact with the wave? Or maybe God had allowed it to happen to prevent something else. After all, one of the golden rules in tropical water is: no bling. Shiny objects attract predators like barracuda. From then on, the watch stayed tucked up under the wetsuit of my right thigh.

The hole I'd dug through the master stateroom mattress in an effort to hang onto it was getting larger. The soft foam used in the construction was ripping with each steep wave and whitecap. The progression of the tearing was gradual and steady from trying to hang on as the waves sharply jerked my body in the opposite direction of the mattress.

I noticed what appeared to be a foot long white and red tube in a wave about forty yards up-sea from Captain Eric and I. It looked like a handheld flare, but I could not tell for sure. If the object was a flare, it could be the one that saves our lives. Our eventual rescue had to be a certainty, because if I died, God would not get the glory for the amazing miracle.

We needed to get a fix on the red and white tube floating up-sea.

"Hey Eric, I just caught a glimpse of what looked like a flare. It was about forty yards up-sea from us." My eyes were locked onto the section of the sea with the same intensity as someone looking for a lost contact lens.

After fifteen minutes of both eyes drilling the rising and falling waves, Eric yelled out, "There, it is a flare."

"I don't know if it's good or bad, Cap, but I think I need to get it."

"All right, Buddy. Unhook yourself and go get it," Eric replied.

The forty yards seemed more like two hundred yards with all the extra distance created by the waves. The loops and hooks of the Velcro started to separate as I pulled the tab until my wrist and was released from the collar. I watched in the direction of the flare and waited to get a fix on its location. After several minutes, there it was. I locked onto it and started a crawl stroke in its general direction with a hope it would not be a waste of valuable energy.

Once again, the seawater was falling off my arms and the splashes were blowing into my eyes and mouth as I thrusted myself forward with every pull of my arms and kick of my legs. This time, there was a soreness in my muscles that hadn't been there earlier in the day. Going up the waves was like trying to climb a twenty-foot straight slide at the park on my belly. Upon reaching the crest, I would search for the small red and white tube of salvation.

After about ten or fifteen minutes, I finally reached the tube. I had great anxiety as I reached out to grab the lone floating flare. Was this a good one that had escaped from the faulty container? Was the end going to have the char from burning, or would there be a red plastic cap protecting the flare from accidental ignition? My right hand locked onto it and I lifted it to see—it was good!

I immediately looked in Captain Eric's direction and began to scream. "It's good! It's good! This isn't one we used!" The anxiety boiling over in my soul did an immediate about face and turned into immense joy with the thought of the saving light the flare could produce. I was overwhelmed with excitement—until I saw the extreme change of expression on Eric's face.

Eric began screaming something to me with his right arm shaking in the air. I couldn't distinguish any of the words launching from his vocal cords and out of his mouth. The wind seemed to be blowing every word he spoke right past his own ears and then behind him. Why was he so frantically yelling? Was he being attacked by a shark? *Does he see a shark?*

With flare in hand, I mustered up every bit of strength and started digging my way through the sea back toward the captain. The very wind and waves that made it impossible to understand Eric's message were now helping to push my body toward him. The closer we came together, the better I could hear him until finally I was able to interpret the cause of his excitement.

When we were about twenty-five yards apart I heard, "It's a fishboat! It's a fishboat! We need the flare!"

Jesus could not have run on water any faster than I swam to Eric. Upon reaching him, I quickly righted myself and popped off the protective cap while turning to my left to see a white sportfishing boat with black accent stripe and a tuna tower about three-quarters of a mile away. The boat was about to pass us. I crashed the striker of the flare against the ignition cap as Captain Eric was in the process of reaching toward the tube that was erupting with red flame and smoke. Like an Olympian passing the baton, Eric took the flare, held it up, and waved it as high as he could.

I lunged to the back of the surfboard bag with arms outstretched. I grabbed the zipper and yanked it open to retrieve the twelve-gauge flare gun with the last remaining bullet. Then I catapulted up onto the surfboard with legs straddling over each side and squeezing to lock on. In almost unison, the hammer of the pistol was cocked and the barrel was broken down to insert the twelve-gauge aerial signal. I fixed my eyes on the passing boat. It appeared to be a fifty-foot Bertram Sportfishing boat. The round was loaded, the barrel closed, and the hammer cocked, and my right index finger was on the trigger waiting for the perfect time to squeeze.

It was critical to perfectly time squeezing the trigger to fire off the flare. When the boat came off a wave and splashed into the next, there was a wall of sea spray that would come up and strike the curtain at the front of bridge. Then the spray would go down the sides of the curtains. When this happened, the captain would be blinded and unable to see our flare. The boat was running at a very slow cruise due to the terrible conditions. It was almost next to us now. I would have to fire on an arch off his bow when the spray cleared and the boat was on the rise. My hand was solidly gripped to the pistol in the setting sun of our final chance. I waited.

Blackwater Baptist Church

This is the last photograph taken of the sportfishing vessel, *Anhinga*, before she was struck by the rogue wave ninety miles at sea from Key West, Florida.

CHAPTER 12:

SAVED BY GRACE!

The orange, Orion, short, twelve-gauge, plastic pistol was pointed toward the sky in a high ready position. The opportunity presented itself as the bow was starting to rise on the next wave and the spray was falling off the curtains. I squeezed the black trigger, releasing the cocked hammer that allowed the firing pin to thrust forward into the primer of the only remaining flare. The flaming projectile departed the muzzle and began sailing through the air in a perfect arch off the Bertram's starboard front quarter. It was a moment of absolute bliss.

Captain Eric and I watched the red fireball reach the optimal height. Out of nowhere, there was a second boat. We heard the distinctive sound of marine diesel engines at a fuel saving slow-cruise directly behind us. I quickly turned around to look up. It was the stem of a very large Viking Sportfish with an enclosed flybridge that was making its way directly over top of the position Eric and I were located. There was a moment of intense fear as I thought, *Dear Lord, no! We've endured so much out here fighting for our lives. Now we're going to be chopped up by this boat's enormous propellers as it runs us over.*

The very front and center bow was aimed directly at us. Our position was at their twelve o'clock or zero degrees. It all happened in an instant. They must have been a few hundred feet away. It was not enough time to dash off to either side of the approaching meat grinder. Regardless, I was not going to leave my captain behind to save myself.

All of a sudden, I could hear the glorious sound of engine RPMs reducing as they dropped back to the humming of low idle revolutions. The bow hovered like a skyscraper as it settled down into the water as she coasted toward Captain Eric and me in neutral.

With arms stretched out, I fell back off the saturated surfboard, splashing into the water like a half Nestea Plunge. In that moment, all of the emotions that had been tucked away and hidden behind the mask of survival hit me to the core. We were rescued! We were saved! Maybe it was because the adrenaline subsided. I don't know, but a flood of tears and wailing poured out of me from the depths of my soul.

This time our emotion was short-lived, because the massive Viking Yacht had stopped with bow directly in front of us, then she began to spin around to disclose her identity. I could see the mate cockpit, which was the lowest deck over the water. He was standing by in the rear corner of the starboard side. Many sportfishing boats had a tuna door in the transom or the rear wall at the very back of the boat. This tuna door can be opened to drag large fish from the sea directly into the boat. It's on the rear of the boat outside of the transom where the name and port of call for the vessel are painted.

The captain left the control located inside of the flybridge enclosure and began operating the vessel from the exterior control station. I remember the sound of the motors' RPMs increasing and the black smoke pouring out of the exhaust as the propellers thrusted and cavitated in an effort to overcome the advisory level winds and seas. The transom was facing us now. It was the *Ditch Digger*, a seventy-two-foot Viking sportfishing boat built in New Gretna, New Jersey. Performing this maneuver was a little dangerous because in doing so, the captain had to time his spin with the swells to prevent the boat from getting caught side-to in a large swell, which could capsize her. He also had to time the position he was in front of us so the wind would blow the boat toward us. The wrong timing of this could have resulted in Eric and me becoming fish food if the propellers chopped us up. The captain performed the spin perfectly.

The surfboard was pushed over to Eric. He positioned himself on the board, and we started making our way toward the back right corner of the *Ditch Digger* as it was drifting back toward us. The mate was making his way around the starboard corner of the transom to reach down and unlock the large stainless-steel handle that holds the tuna door closed. Most mates have lost a few fish, a gaff, or scrub brush from this door accidentally opening sometime in their career. I recognized the mate from the previous year in Mexico at the Hacienda Delmar Dock as he was preparing the door for his next big catch. Eric and I kicked toward our new heroes. All of a sudden, as I approached the opening of the tuna door, a large passing wave washed me right into the boat. I went right past the mate and halfway across the cockpit as he was reaching for me. Like a large fish rolling on deck until slowing to a stop.

I had an overwhelming feeling of guilt for boarding the rescuing vessel before my captain. Overcome with an enormous adrenaline rush, I jumped up, spun around, and rushed to the stern, rudely pushing the mate across the cockpit to get back to Eric. Without hesitation, I was fully prepared to make the running leap up onto the covering board and dive back into the restless waves of the foaming deep to get to Eric. What a shocker that would have been for the crew of the *Ditch Digger* to see the guy they just found floating ninety nautical miles out in the middle of nowhere turn around and jump back in the water!

Seasoned mates are masters of rapidly maneuvering around in the cockpit, just as rodeo clowns are masters of the arena. Although I had never been in this particular cockpit before, I would have had no problem making the dash up and over the covering boards to get to Eric. Countless times, I had made the running leap up onto the stern's covering boards at the back of a rolling and pitching boat. The purpose was to gain an elevated position to see how the baits were pulling through the water as the boat was trolling. It was my signature move for the slow days while charter fishing. As charter fishermen, we practically sold action, so when the fish had tight lips, we had to make our own action to bedazzle the customers. Similar to a bartender throwing a bottle of rum around his back and catching it in one hand while pouring it into the glass with the other. The move was usually good for an extra twenty in the tip jar at the end of the day. I only went too far once—okay, twice—falling into water washing behind the boat. Captain Dave and Captain Jimmy were not pleased with this particular performance, but the charter passengers sure thought it was funny. Like I said, we sold action.

By the time I was in position, the wave that had altered the plan for boarding the rescue vessel had long passed. Eric was near the transom. I don't know where it came from but

I had never before had such a feeling of paternal instinctiveness. Eric was now getting within reach. Soon he was there with his left hand grasping the actual tuna door, which has hinges on the inboard side to allow it to swing folding back to latch against the stern in the locked open position. His right arm was draped fully across the top of the board as his body drew nearer to the opening. He was only moments away from escaping the clutches of the monster that had tried valiantly to overcome us.

The cockpit deck height just inside the tuna door was about a foot above the water line. I could finally grab ahold of Captain Eric and pull him through the opening to safety. When he let go of the surfboard, I pulled him onto the deck with a grasp tighter than any arm wrestler. It was over. *Thank you, Jesus, for your great mercy and grace shed upon this unworthy man, and Captain Eric too!*

Eric looked at me and said, "Johnny, I'm sorry I couldn't hang onto your surfboard." I was surprised to hear him so emotionally crushed. I have never heard such a heartfelt apology in my life. Maybe because he knew surfboards were expensive. For the first time since the battle for survival had started, Eric and I were not in agreement. At that moment, the surfboard seemed to be the most insignificant thing on the face of the earth to me. We would see home again, and I'd had an encounter with the creator of the universe! That was priceless and worth more than every surfboard on the earth.

It was finally a perfect time for a confession. I broke the news to Eric about the surfboard's condition all along, the defeating truth I hadn't let him know earlier. "Eric, don't worry about the surfboard. It was broken in the bag anyway." The slight smile and sigh of relief that escaped him made me grin.

Not once during the entire time of the struggle was there ever a moment or even feeling of blame toward each other. As Captain Steve used to always say, "It is what it is." It was what it was for Eric and me. The situation we were just rescued from had been 100 percent out of our control. Often in life, we enter struggles either by our own bad choices or through a trial that has been put into our lives. Our struggles can be in marriage, at work, with a relative, or with a friend. If we don't look for blame, we won't find it.

Once both of us were onboard, my emotional baggage struck hard, and what little bit of water was left in my body was pouring out my eyes. I cannot say they were all tears of happiness. There were tears of absolute exhaustion from dehydration and hypothermia. Others were tears of the physical pain throughout my body from the fight. I would say that most were tears of gratitude because by faith the Lord is true to save.

Most sportfishing boats are operated from the helm on the flybridge directly above the main salon. The Ditch Digger had a flybridge in the same location, but it was fully enclosed with solid walls, glass windows, a door, and a spiral stairwell that connected to the main salon. The mate guided Eric and I into the main salon. This was the first time in eleven hours we had protection from one of the most unforgiving environments on earth. We had experienced a lot since early that morning when fixing the salon door and crawling out of the sea just before dark. It was the first time Eric had been in shelter since we left before sunrise at five o'clock. Shelter is one of the basic necessities of survival for human beings.

Once we were inside and out of the elements, the next struggle began. The detailed memories of many events became nonexistent. My body was starting to go into the next phase, which was possibly more life-threatening than being in the water. Things were fading in and out as my body started to go into shock. During the course of my education to become a safety engineer, we had to understand the effects of various types of traumas on the human body. Based on my training, in a surreal way, I knew what was going on. Typically, a person going into shock does not realize what's happening to them.

I remember Eric and myself being wrapped in towels and John, the Captain of the *Ditch Digger*, coming down the spiral stair case to the salon to check on us. As any good seafaring captain, his first gracious offer to new passengers was a drink of rum. Eric and I both had a chuckle over this kind offer. We both replied, "No, thank you. Water, please. We need water." Oh how wonderful it was to put crystal clear, pure water to our lips and swallow. It was as if it was absorbed by our body before ever reaching our bellies. I remember it feeling so refreshing and light versus the heavy dehydrating seawater invading my mouth over those many hours.

The mate was kindly off gathering dry clothes for us to warm our bodies. Considering they'd picked us up while in route to the Yucatan of Mexico, I have no idea where he found Eric and I each a brown sweatshirt and a pair of jeans. It didn't matter; they were dry. They fit Eric pretty good, but at six feet tall, mine didn't fit so well. I remember lying there on the floor with pant cuffs at mid-shin and sweatshirt sleeve cuffs at mid-forearm. It provided a well-needed source of laughter. Despite my exposed limbs, all I felt was gratefulness toward the kindness of our heroes. To be discovered by an American-registered Viking Yacht was an absolute blessing, but I guess beggars can't be choosers. We would have climbed aboard any boat from any country.

I also remember the stunned look on Captain John's face as he recognized he had just rescued his good friend Eric. He recounted the day's events for the *Ditch Digger* and *Sans Souci*. They had left later in the day with the standard plan of making a two-day crossing. Once they were out in the Gulf Stream, they realized how bad the sea conditions were getting, so they altered their course to run southern toward Cuba. Once closer to Cuba and out of the strong Gulf Stream current, they would alter to a westerly course, running parallel to the shore of Cuba until they arrived at the western tip of the island. They would then alter course again more southwesterly to Isla Mujeres, Mexico.

Size and speed are two major factors when trying to make way in rough sea conditions. Captains often work together to soften the ride by having a larger boat run in front of a smaller boat to knock down the waves. The larger boat would adjust to a slower speed to a level comfortable for the following vessel.

This is exactly what had happened with the *Ditch Digger* and *San Souci*. The heavier seventy-two-foot Viking was in front smashing down the waves for the following Bertram that was twenty-two feet shorter. They ran in this follow-the-leader fashion until they started to see debris in the water. Not certain what had happened to cause so much random trash, they separated to run side-by-side about three quarters of a mile apart. Captain John said when he first saw us in the water, he thought we might be refugees escaping Cuba. That is, until he saw our white faces. Following this brief conversation, he exited the salon via the narrow spiral stairs and went back up to take command of the helm.

It is difficult to describe in words the following hours as Eric and I lay on the salon floor in the dark, rumbling vibrations of the diesel engines directly below us reassuring our safety. We were no longer lost in the open sea. We chatted briefly as our hearts were filled with gratitude about the latest of the amazing miracle we had experienced. What if we hadn't spotted the floating flare? Maybe we would have been in a slightly different location. We could have been off to the side of the *Ditch Digger* as it passed by us.

I remember lying there on the floor uncontrollably shivering, fully exhausted but unable sleep. It was like sounds were muffled, including when others were talking. I really wanted to be at peace sleeping, but I could not do it. Every time I closed my eyes and started to doze off, my dreams went right back into the terror I had just escaped. I just laid there staring at some sort of fixture on the ceiling, feeling mindless as I slipped deeper and deeper into some form of shock.

Finally, I did fall asleep sometime in the early morning hours at around three o'clock. After a couple hours, I woke up and proceeded up the spiral staircase to the bridge where Eric and John were catching up on old times. Eric was sitting in the companion chair on the port side of the helms chair where the captain was behind the wheel. I sat down on the bench to the right of Captain John and peered out the front windshield, across the bow, and out to the horizon.

"Not too much farther to go," said the captain.

After a while, Eric leaned forward and looked over toward me while seated in the companion chair. I couldn't figure out the mischievous look on his face until he said, "Happy Birthday, buddy!" In the midst of the roaring seas, facing impending death, my date of birth had been the furthest thing on my mind.

Cuba was behind us. We knew it wasn't much farther when Isla Contoy and Isla Mujeres started to become visible on the *Ditch Digger*'s long-range radar. Captain Eric and I would soon experience a new joy of stepping on land in Mexico.

A frustrating thought nagged at me. How would we be able to clear customs and immigrations in a foreign country without passports or any other documents to prove who we were?

CHAPTER 13:

A FATHER'S LOVE

I remember feeling out of place and lethargic as the *Ditch Digger* pulled up to the Hacienda Del Mar dock. As we parked side-to on the main dock, I stared at the unique dark-grained ironwood planks. A memory from the previous year of my friend, Pancho, telling me the wood was so hard they had to predrill every hole for each nail that would be driven in to secure the timbers together floated through my consciousness. My blank stare was evidence of the acute stress disorder that was manifesting itself in my mind.

The news about the fate of the *Anhinga* and its crew had been reported via the Ship to Shore communications shortly after we were discovered. The story of the miraculous event had spread quickly from Mexico all the way to Virginia Beach. As we initially approached the dock, there were only a few people awaiting our arrival. A steady stream of fishermen began to approach as the mooring lines of the *Ditch Digger* were secured. This gathering was a familiar feeling to the days on the charter boat dock when anxious crowds shifted from boat to boat as we returned to see the daily catches.

I had been blessed over the years to experience the crowd on the dock awaiting our return with a big catch. With awe and joy, they cheered as boom extended over, the hoist was lowered into the cockpit, the rigging was connected, and magnificent fish were raised for all to see. Next, we gathered around the prize with a proud pose for the photo to document the event. There was no formal Hall of Fame where all the pictures of great fish could be seen, but there are numerous places where the photos are displayed. These Walls of Fame could be in a restaurant, office, or even in a home on the refrigerator.

There were no cheers for this arrival. The facial expressions on the dock were not of joy. Looks of uncertainty passed between people as they discovered who it was that went down out there. The rumors and good guesses were satisfied when they saw foreign crew aboard the *Ditch Digger*. Many knew Eric was the captain of the *Anhinga* for years. We had been so busy and my position on the boat was so recent that the news Eric hired me hadn't spread. It had to have been clear to bystanders I was one of the crew members fished from the sea by the looks of my clothes being two sizes too small.

I was overwhelmed with a feeling of security the moment my right foot made contact with the predrilled ironwood dock as I stepped off the seventy-two-foot Viking. The shivering from the beginning states of hypothermia were exchanged for the blazing Cancún heat. It always seemed to be hotter in the developed area of Cancún than in the jungle surrounding Puerto Aventuras. The bright Yucatan sun was blinding as I scanned the dock for Meg or Tommy, my friends from home who'd been tied up at Hacienda during the 1997 season. There were many friends and familiar faces, but at that moment I needed to retreat to somewhere with a sense of home.

I was humbled by the greeting line that formed. The line was filled with my brothers who had fished all over the world. The third person I came to was a fishing brother and a soul brother. Scotty and I were bonded by our love for surfing in addition to our love for fishing. Overwhelmed with emotions, fatigued, and still shivering, I stumbled while hugging my friend. I was so thankful to be alive. He had already heard about the surfboard helping to save Eric and me.

Bystanders gaped at us in shock as if they were staring at ghosts. The words were few and the hugs were large. What were the right words to say to someone who'd defied the odds and just experienced a mariner's ultimate nightmare? I heard two crew members I didn't know sum up the whole event in the six simple words: "God saved those boys out there." My mind was a blur as my eyes looked over the crowd of those gathering. "Thank God you two made it." There was no glory in it for Captain Eric or me. We had humble gratitude, because if it hadn't been for God, I was sure we'd have been shark bait. In the moment, as everyone was recognizing where our salvation came from, I refrained from saying a word about the miraculous event that occurred during my suicide attempt.

Following captains and mates continued to greet us. We were humbled. A sense of relief fell upon me when the crew of the *Top Priority* was approaching. The owner was from Richmond, Virginia, and kept his boat in Rudee Inlet. Captain Neil and JW mate had been friends for many years. They are as nice a pair of people as anyone could ever meet. Neil had been a broker of commercial real estate around Richmond, and JW was a heavy crane operator in the Hampton Roads area of Virginia. Both had taken a risk by leaving their careers for their addictive love of offshore fishing. Hearing their voices was so comforting, a taste of home I had longed for while adrift at sea. This was my first time experiencing an overwhelming feeling of home sickness.

The *Top Priority* was a sixty-six-foot Ocean Yacht with a luxurious interior, and she was equipped with about every electronic device on the market. I turned to walk toward the end of the main dock to greet Captain Neil and his mate, JW. We gave each other a man hug. Neil immediately noticed my strain to see in the Mexican sun.

"Johnny. Come on down to the boat. I have a pair of sunglasses for you," JW said.

I replied, "Thank you so much."

I had always been cautious walking down the Hacienda dock. I could break a toe if I missed seeing a gap between two of the ironwood planks while walking to the *Top Priority*. The bare-feet and stubbing your toe warning was the first thing I learned about the dock the previous year. I never could understand how the Mexicans' feet were so tough. Maybe they were conditioned by walking barefoot on the hard and jagged surfaces of the Yucatan jungles.

We stepped aboard the *Top Priority* with our toes still intact. Neil opened the door and invited me in with the essence of a true Virginian gentleman. I entered and had to sit down on the absorbing cushions of the salon couch. It was a moment of peace as I leaned back with my eyes closed. I became saturated in the feeling of being at home. My body melted into the leather as all the emotions stored inside seemed to let go for a brief couple of minutes. Of course, it was not home, but it was as close as I could get for the moment.

Captain Neil opened a drawer and passed JW a pair of black-framed sunglasses. JW passed them to me. As I reached, I recognized the brand and model of the glasses, which provided an additional level of the needed comfort. They were Ravens.

In the comfort of silence, I recalled spending time with the whole Arnette Sunglasses staff in San Clemente, California, during the fall. My close friend, Trick, was their motorsports marketing representative. We drove an RV across the country for a premiere of their surf video in Los Angeles. He had done most of the driving, especially after we went through a blizzard in the High Desert as we came across Interstate 40. I had been grateful for the opportunity to drive across the United States. The surfboard from that trip was gone and drifting in the Gulf Stream.

The crew of the *Top Priority* then asked the burning question that was on all of their minds.

"What happened?" the captain asked.

In a fifteen-minute synopsis, I explained how the boat had fallen into a rogue wave and was gone within minutes. I kept the description limited to the brief time frame of the boat actually going down to keep the emotions from pulling me deeper into shock. Then I asked the question that had been deeply burning inside of me.

"May I please use your satellite phone to call my parents?" I asked.

"Certainly," Neil replied. He knew my parents from the many conversations they'd had on the dock as they patiently waited behind the boat's slip after our return from the day's trip offshore in Virginia Beach.

He pushed numbers as I narrated them to him and then passed me the phone. There were so many feelings flowing through me as the phone rang. My father answered. The moment I heard "Hello," tears of joy began to fill my eyes and roll down my cheek.

"Dad. It's me, Johnny. I'm on a satellite phone, so I sound different. It's going to be hard to hear me, and there'll be a delay between our transmission. I am okay, but there's something big I have to tell you."

"All right, go ahead," my father replied in a concerned tone. After all, parents never like to hear the conversation lead-in, "I'm okay, but..."

"Dad, the *Anhinga* is gone. We were hit by a rogue wave ninety miles off the beach..." I explained what had happened as succinctly as possible and let him know my current condition.

He was dumbfounded by what he'd just heard from the mouth of his only son. It was strange to hear him shocked into silence. He has always been very comprehensive of details during serious conversations.

"I don't understand. What did you say, son?"

My father has always been a very loving man toward his family and friends, but tears were few and far between for him. I remember when my grandmother, a very loving and Godly woman, passed away as a result of her battle with cancer. My father cried soundlessly as tears drained from his eyes.

While still on the satellite phone call, I explained to him a second time what had happened. That time, it sunk in. He understood the struggle and trauma his son had survived. Next, I experienced one of the biggest revelations of my life. My father started bawling like a baby. There was a vocal flow of emotions, an eruption of love and pain, as he cried for his son between gasps of air.

It was in that moment when I realized the enormous love a parent has for their children. I got it. The love a parent has for their children must be one of the most powerful forces in all creation. Love is amazing; it has the power to change the world.

Dad was so distraught he backed out of a flounder fishing trip. He'd planned to go to the Eastern Shore of Virginia the next morning with his good friends, Pete and Barry. My father was still crying when he called Pete and told him he couldn't handle going fishing. Dad was too upset to be on the water, the very thing that had almost killed his son. My father was so emotional when he talked to the soil-stained Blackwater Farmer, it made Pete emotional. Then Pete couldn't hold back the tears when he told Barry, "Austin will not be fishing with us." They were an emotional wreck thirteen hundred miles away.

Pete and his wife, Lettie, were like grandparents to me as I grew up running around their farm and in the shadow of Blackwater Hunt Club. They had a hand in developing my love for fishing by allowing me the unique opportunity to fish in the "No Fishing" section of their canal. Maybe that is partially why Pete was crying too.

Before hanging up the phone, my father gave me my sister's phone number. My mom was staying with her in Danville, Virginia, to help out with my three-month-old nephew as my sister transitioned back into her career. The nephew who I had thought twenty-four hours earlier would never get to know his uncle. I was so eternally thankful to Neil and JW for their simple act of kindness of finding a pair of sunglasses and giving me an opportunity to use their phone so I could hear the voices of my family members.

I was then shocked to see two more friends as I walked back toward the seventy-two-foot Viking. I knew their boats were part of the Puerto Aventuras fleet, so they must have been there to see me. JJ from the *Sea Hag* and Kirk from the *Blank Check* went above and beyond when they rented a car to drive over sixty miles from Puerto Aventuras to Cancún. The bag they were holding provided confirmation of a friend's love for a brother. The bag they graciously brought me was filled with a toothbrush, toothpaste, deodorant, and a hair brush. It also included a gray pair of shorts and a really nice button-up teal and white collared shirt.

Then I saw Dickie, who gave me a bear hug, one I'd never experienced the likes of. With his larger-than-life smile, he proclaimed, "I'm glad you made it, buddy."

I don't remember who ended up giving me the shoes I wore, but I was so thankful for them.

So often growing up in small country church, we'd collected donations of toiletries for the poor, migrant workers who would come to Virginia to pick crops during the summer. The experience gave me a new appreciation of providing for the needs of other. Prior to this day, never in my life had I experienced what it was like to have nothing and have your needs be met by the kindness of others. If everyone experienced that, the world would be a kinder place.

I figured it would be best to give Dad a little time to call Mom and let it sink in before I called. An hour later, Jim, the dock master, allowed me to use the marina phone to call my mother. She was overjoyed to know that I was all right. She was no stranger to the dangers of the open sea. When my mother was a girl, my grandfather was a master chief in the US Coast Guard. He'd received orders for Pearl Harbor. While on a ship crossing the Pacific Ocean, my mother had witnessed a rescue on the high seas. The image burned deep into her memories as a little girl.

Her next endeavor was to get her son back home. This was not a simple task, considering Eric and I now had nothing to provide evidence of our citizenship. My mother hoped our local senator could provide assistance in getting us back into the country.[1]

---

1   Thank you to everyone who showed such great love and support after our rescue. Due to shock, I was unable to recall all of the acts of kindness. Such as, the Virginia Beach based Pursuer canceling their charter to be waiting at the dock for me to arrive.

The family at Disney World in 2016. Being on dry land in Mexico was better than being at Disney World.

CHAPTER 14:

RETURNING HOME

We were going to need some political influence to secure our reentry into the United States. Eric and I did not have so much as a passport, driver's license, or even a library card to say who we were. Our proof of identity had gone down with the *Anhinga*. We were fortunate to have loved ones who wanted us home. One was my mother who contacted a local senator. Senator Owen Pickett went to work helping to secure the process of painlessly getting us back into the United States.

The effort to get Captain Eric and me home was paying off as an American came walking across a thatch-grass awning with what appeared to be two letters in hand. This person had a presence of authority and certainly was not dressed to go fishing. We discovered it was the ambassador from the US Embassy and Consulates. The envelopes contained letters for Eric and me to present to Customs and Immigration agents when we returned to the United States. We were very fortunate to have our much-needed letters of passage delivered to the marina.

That night, I had one of the most memorable birthday dinners I have ever had. Jim and his wife, from Hacienda

Del Mar Marina, treated Eric and me to a fabulous Italian restaurant in town. I had the best veal marsala to ever touch my tongue. This was the first time Eric and I would share the story in detail at the same time.

Following dinner, we returned to the marina. One part of me wanted to go out on the strip in Cancún. Yet, another side of my soul wanted nothing to do with stepping back into partying like a rock star. The wiser side prevailed. I was still physically and emotionally drained of all energy. I went to bed that night anticipating that Captain Eric and I would be flying back to the States in the morning.

I was so glad when the sun started to rise. The nightmares ceased with the morning light. When Eric and I realized we didn't have so much as a suitcase or duffle bag to put our belongings in for the flight home, the crew of the *Ditch Digger* searched desperately for some sort of luggage. They didn't have any luck, but they were able to provide us with the next best thing—a trash compactor bag. It was perfect. It was tough, could be easily closed, and would fit in the overhead compartment.

We loaded our torn life jackets and the clothes we were wearing when the *Anhinga* went down into the compactor bag, then we were off to Cancún International Airport with our letters in hand. Eric and I must have certainly looked strange walking through the airport with all of our belongings in a rectangular extra-heavy trash bag. But our appearance was the least of our worries. We just wanted to get home to our families.

The loud speaker announced our boarding. We had not checked to see where on the plane we would be sitting other than to make sure we'd be sitting next to each other. After shuffling our way almost halfway toward the back of the plane, we found our seat numbers on the right side. Eric placed our street person luggage in the overhead storage as I had the misfortune of the window seat. I had to close the shade. The last thing I wanted to see was water we just came out of all the way to Florida.

We were so excited to get back home that we hardly noticed the extra leg room our seats provided. Then, a flight attendant stepped into the extra leg space to allow boarding passengers to pass in the aisle. Then it hit me. *She is not really going to say it, is she? She is!* In a sweet and comforting voice, the flight attendant began her well-rehearsed safety message.

"Hello, gentlemen. You're sitting in an emergency exit row. In the event of an emergency landing, are you willing and able to assist with the evacuation of the plane?"

Captain Eric and I just looked at each other and laughed. "Yes, ma'am," we replied.

We were both thinking the same thing. *"Lady, if you only knew what we've just gone through, you'd know anything that could possibly happen on this plane would be no problem."*

On the other hand, she was probably thinking, *"I don't see what's so funny. Sheesh, I hope our lives don't actually end up depending on these jerks."*

As we were flying home, I couldn't help but look out the window and wonder if spotting us from that altitude would have been possible. I remember thinking, *"I hope we're not flying past anyone down there in need of salvation."* I wondered if the orange smoke had as much contrast as the whitecaps did against the backdrop of the deep blue.

It was so amazing to think we were actually on our way home. Seeing the ocean below us and imagining what we had survived was even more humbling. Eric and I spent some of the plane ride talking about how there was no other way to explain what had happened other than a miracle. Without a doubt, it was divine intervention. The conversation pulsed in a moment of personal reflection for each of us, and I wondered if I should tell Captain Eric what had really happened on that second trip out for the EPIRB. I felt like I was hiding something really important from him.

Then Eric looked straight into my eyes and said, "Buddy, I truly believe." In that moment, everything we had experienced while lost at sea was absolutely worth the struggle. I grew up listening to a preacher say, "There is nothing on this earth more precious than a person believing that Jesus died on the cross for our forgiveness." Captain Eric's father was a preacher who would have said the same. I believed, too, but I was too afraid to reveal what had happened when we separated. Maybe I just wasn't mature enough to understand it yet.

Stepping off the plane and onto the gate ramp at the Miami Airport was surreal. Finally, we were back on US ground. Our flight was an international one that required Captain Eric and me to proceed directly to US Immigration and Customs. We rounded the corner into the large room with our fashionable trash compactor bag luggage. A mass of people were standing in lines with their passports and driver's licenses in hand, ready to present them to the agents. Each of the many lines seemed to be one hundred fifty to two hundred feet long. As great of a hassle as this appeared to be, I was grateful to have returned to the greatest country in the world.

Eric and I stood at the back of the room looking somewhat dumbfounded as we analyzed the lines to see which would be the best selection. While standing there, we were suddenly approached by a uniformed gentleman wearing a gold badge.

"Are you Captain Eric Bingham and First Mate John Savage?" the agent asked.

"Yes, sir, that is us," Eric replied as we both tightly pinched our envelopes between our fingers.

"Follow me," he said with authority as he began walking off to the right of the crowded lines. The agent proceeded to an empty turnstile. He stopped, and with an about-face he said, "May I see your letters?"

Eric was in front, so he handed the agent his envelope.

Before even opening the letter, he stopped and looked at Eric and me with deep compassion, saying, "Gentlemen, I am sorry to hear about what you went through. I'm glad you all made it back alive."

It was a struggle to hold back the tears of gratitude.

He opened Eric's envelope, and after a quick glance at the piece of paper, he opened the gate and said, "Welcome home."

"Thank you," we replied. As I passed through the gate, I attempted to give him the envelope that I had been protecting for the past twenty-four hours with the same determination as a sentinel protecting the Tomb of the Unknown Solider.

"You are fine. I don't need it," the agent said as I stepped on the US citizen side of the gate.

Captain Eric and I proceeded to the concourse where Eric's wife, Lisa, and my Uncle Joe were waiting.

When I saw Uncle Joe my heart was so filled with emotions of what I had been longing for—family. There are some voids in life that can only be filled by a family member. Exhausted and in shock, Captain Eric and I separated for the first time since I paddled back to him for the miraculous reunion.

Joe could tell I had experienced something amazing. We stayed up late that night as my uncle listened to me revisiting the highs and lows of the struggle two days prior. Uncle Joe was certain that whatever had happened out there had placed an unshakable faith within me. The next morning, he graciously dropped me off at the airport.

Out of habit, I stopped by the Palm Beach Airport gift shop before boarding the plane. *Marlin, Salt Water Sportsman,* and *Sport Fishing* were my regular magazines of choice. This day was different. I knew exactly what book I wanted. I wanted the book Eric had just read before we left for Mexico. I walked right past the magazine rack and over to the bookshelf. I wanted to find out what happened to the swordfisherman. I scanned the rows until I found the red trim and black-and-white picture of waves I was looking for. The cover represented my battle to survive three days prior. The author must have researched to find out the things Eric and I knew; the things we did not talk about. The book told the story of what happened to the crew of the swordfishing boat *Andrea Gail.* The name of the book was *The Perfect Storm,* by Sebastian Junger. I bought the book and a highlighter so I could make note of similarities.

I was so excited to get back home and see the family and friends I never thought I would see again. My mom was able to book me a flight from West Palm Beach International Airport to Norfolk International Airport. The general seating on the airplane was full. After hearing about why I needed an emergency flight home, the airline sold my mother a first-class flight for the price of general seating. This time, my clothes were not in a trash compactor bag. They were in an actual suitcase.

When I arrived at my window seat, I tried to avoid the thought of another flight looking over the sea. But this time, the seat was amazingly comfortable. I was staring into the cockpit of the plane wondering the differences between marine and aviation electronics when a very well-dressed gentleman said, "Hello," as he opened the overhead baggage locker to stow his briefcase.

The well-dressed, strange man was very polite as we both introduced ourselves. We had some small talk until the flight attendant began her safety briefing. The plane was then taxied to the runway, and off we went. I looked out the window and saw the beautiful blue water of the Gulf Stream. On average, Palm Beach is the closest point the Gulf Stream comes to land of anywhere in the United States. Since I wasn't exactly feeling chatty at the time, I used the plane ride as an opportunity to retreat into my recent purchase.

My highlighter was at the ready as I was drawn into the story Mr. Junger had so creatively illustrated with words. Every other paragraph or so, the words would be covered with neon lime-green and a note or two written in the margin of the page. I could sense the eyes of my neighbor locking on the pages I was noting like a textbook. My emotions were building to the point I had to close the pages to escape from the storm.

The neighbor and I resumed the small talk we started after boarding. He disclosed he was heading to his home in New York City. I informed him I was a charter fisherman on the way home to see my family. He asked about the book I was reading and marking as if it were a college textbook. He correctly sensed the importance with which I was documenting my journey through the novel.

I began to share the story of how God performed an undeniable miracle saving the crew of the *Anhinga*. He listened intensely as tears began to roll down his cheeks. The pilot then asked for seatbelts to be fastened as our descent to

Norfolk International Airport began. What happened next would be my first experience observing the power of the story of the *Anhinga*.

The stranger sitting in first class next to me then unveiled more about himself. With watery eyes, he informed me he was the president and CEO of a very large chemical company in the United States and served on the board of directors for several chemical companies in Europe of which he had financial interest. He was on his way to his home in New York City that night, and then he had to fly to Europe for a board meeting. We could hear the landing-gear bay doors open as we were on final approach to Norfolk International Airport. He looked into my eyes surrounded by a sea and sun-battered face.

"When I was getting out of college, I had nothing to my name. I went overseas with the Peace Corps. I served others who were in great need. I was filled with joy and peace by helping others. The way this economy is going, I could lose everything I own in the snap of a finger. And do you know what? It really doesn't matter, because me and my family are alive and healthy."

The plane we were on would be continuing on to his final destination in New York. It stopped at the gate, and the doors could be heard opening as people began to shuffle.

"It was a pleasure meeting you, sir," I said.

The well-dressed stranger replied, "Thank you very much for sharing your story with me. I will be having dinner with my daughter tonight in the city. I'm going to share this incredible story with her."

He then thanked me again for sharing the story. My heart was warmed. I could tell God had used my story to touch the core of this wealthy man's soul.

The moment my feet touched the gateway at Norfolk International, it was surreal. I was back home in Virginia. I had trouble containing my emotions when I spotted my parents through the sea of travelers and soldiers. I wanted to cry and shout for joy at the same time. The feeling was the same for them. I soon fell back into the reclusion of shock. There would have been no peace for them if I had been forever lost in the Gulf Stream.

As we were approaching home, I looked out the left window for another surreal moment. It was Blackwater Baptist Church. The gratefulness for the great thing God had done was dulled by my lethargic state, but I recalled the stillness in my soul that came from singing "Amazing Grace" and "Just as I Am" while fighting for life in the middle of the wind and waves.

The hot pink flowers of the Crepe Myrtles lining my parents' driveway greeted us as we pulled in. I had never thought I would see the darkened cedar-sided home again. My sister and brother-in-law soon arrived with my nephew. The nephew I had held as a newborn before leaving for the season. The nephew I was certain I'd never see grow up.

We cherished the day together as a family. The very nature of the gathering prompted a visit with my grandfather, who lived next door. My mother wanted to document the moment of four generations in film. We were scattered all around the living room. The picture included my grandfather, father, baby Michael, and me. After the photo, I shared a few fishing stories with my grandfather until I was too exhausted to continue. The pain was too great to share the details of the beast that had almost wrecked my life. The shock was still taking its toll.

My heart was filled after spending a couple days with my family, but it had been months since I had slept in my bed. I had not seen my roommate since he came to Palm Beach to get ideas for a new bar he was building upstairs in his family's restaurant. Aunt Donna and Uncle Joe always welcomed my friends with a place to stay when they came to visit.

I needed to be alone for a little while so I could lay in my bedroom and cry. I borrowed Mom's Cherokee and went home. Mike and I lived in a second floor, two-bedroom condo on Rudee Inlet that he bought from his uncle who developed the complex. No one was home when I arrived. I wanted to let the emotions leak out of me in tears, but the shock wouldn't let me do it. My emotions were held captive by the fear that had oppressed my soul. The rogue wave and the fight to survive had scared me to death. I also had an intense feeling of guilt for being alive. In my heart, I knew there were others in this world who deserved to be saved but were not.

A few hours later, Mike came through the door. In an instant, one person who was never at a loss for words just stood there staring at me. My swollen face was covered in scales from the intense exposure to the elements, and my eyes must have appeared black because of my dilated pupils. I knew he had not heard the whole story, as the full details had not yet reached the Rudee Inlet fleet. Through all of the superficial scars, he could tell something amazing had happened to me. Prior to hearing the details of the story, my best friend sensed the supernatural had happened. He knew I'd had an experience with God.

We sat in our den as I told him the story from beginning to end. After digesting my story for a while, Mike said, "We're going out," in a matter-of-fact tone. He made it clear that he had decided if anyone needed a night out on the town, it was his sea-battered buddy. We headed out to the clubs just over the bridge on the Virginia Beach Oceanfront strip. An amazing transformation occurred that night while we were out. I came out of my state of shock. The numbing effect of the alcohol wasn't what brought on the transformation, it was the love of my friends.

After a few hours, we headed back to the condo because I had to be up early the next morning to catch a flight to Palm Beach. The boat owner had been doing his best to provide Captain Eric and me with valuable time at home, but the insurance company was demanding our presence for a deposition. I had to hurry back to Palm Beach. I was about to learn how heartless a human could be.

Me holding baby nephew (Michael), who I never thought I would see again. The effects of the exposure are visible in this photo taken five days after being pulled from the sea. Notice the lacerations on my forehead from impacts with surface debris as the wind and waves increased.

CHAPTER 15:

THE DEPOSITION

I was able to get a couple hours of sleep before my alarm went off at 5:30 a.m. My parents were dropping me off at the airport. The smell of the alcohol coming out of my pores must have been fumigating them. Mike had accomplished his mission and crushed me. If I'm dumb, I'd better be tough. After hugs and kisses from Mom and Dad, I was off to meet the need of the insurance company. As soon the plane was in the air, I tried to take a nap. I wasn't looking forward to landing and being forced to relive and tell the story the next morning. I really just wanted to put it far from my mind.

Having never been through a deposition before, I guessed it might be like the incident investigation process we learned in Safety Program Management Class. They would be interviewing us separately to see if our stories matched. Our stories could never perfectly match because we were separated for so much of the time while I was looking for the EPIRB. I figured it would be cut and dry with a few questions and then we would be able to go get lunch. Common sense said we hadn't sunk the boat on purpose—ninety miles offshore in the Gulf Stream... without a distress call, EPIRB, or life raft. No one would do that.

The next morning, I met Eric at the insurance company's office. He didn't look very happy about the process, either. We checked in with the receptionist and had a seat. They called the captain in. Eric was the first to go into the conference room to be interrogated. I sat in the lobby staring at the door, wondering what was happening in there.

However, after much time had passed since Eric had started their little question-and-answer session, I began to wonder if the ludicrousness of the idea we'd sunk the *Anhinga* was as apparent to them. My palms became clammy as I began to get nervous thinking about how I could accurately describe the size and power of the monstrous wave. For centuries, crazy things have been happening to mariners at sea. Our experience was one of them, and Eric and I should have been drowned at the bottom of the sea.

What was happening in there with my captain? It was almost as if the walls were soundproof. I could hear nothing of the conversation.

Then, similar to waiting in the examination room at the doctor's office, I began to hear noises on the other side of the door. The handle was turning. I could hear the latch bolt as it retreated from the strike plate. As the door began to open, there was an ever so slight creaking of the hinges. Eric walked out with an appearance of rigidness I had never seen before. It was very obvious my captain was angry.

Captain Eric had not even gotten mad at me the night of the *Anhinga* salon dance party in Chub Cay. The boss's daughter and I were in and out of the boat keeping him up all hours of the night as we made more rum drinks. The next day, we went tournament fishing, and I truly struggled to keep up with the baits. I had certainly deserved to be fired, yet captain Eric hadn't been angry with me at all. The boss's wife seemed to be laughing about my fumbling. She was probably thinking, *If you're dumb, you better be tough.*

Staying up late and drinking a little bit too much the night before a tournament was a terrible thing to do. So I could not imagine what had Eric so fired up.

A good captain and mate team learn how to communicate without words. The look on my captain's face told the story of several emotions at one time. He had a look of anger from something that happened in the room during the questioning. Was it possible they questioned his authority or seamanship abilities? I made a note to make sure they heard how great a seaman and captain Eric was. Pain was also present in the palette of emotions on Eric's face, most likely from reliving the horrific story to satisfy their request for information. Most striking was the protective look of concern. Concern for what I was about to experience.

As the captain cleared the doorway, he gave those in the room behind him orders to take it easy on me.

"John Savage. It's your turn. Come in," the man inside the room said.

As Eric and I approached each other, I could see there was also a dampness to his eyes.

When we passed each other close enough to brush elbows, Captain Eric leaned over and whispered, "Buddy, if it gets too hard, you don't have to."

"I can do it, Cap," I replied.

I walked into the conference room as one gentleman shut the door behind me. Another man was already sitting at the table with various papers in front of him. The gentleman who greeted me at the door then proceeded to the far side of the table and sat down next to the other man. I was invited to sit across from them.

The man who'd greeted me introduced himself. The conversation went something like this:

"Hi, John. My name is Phil, and I'm an adjuster with the insurance company that provided the coverage for the *Anhinga*. I am very sorry to hear about your experience. We'll be asking you a series of questions related to the events associated with how the *Anhinga* sunk. Before we get started, is there anything I can get for you? Would you like a water?"

"No, sir. I'm good," I replied with a light chuckle. Being offered water had taken on a whole new meaning for me because now I realized how precious it is. For the rest of my life, I would think about the moment when Eric and I were pulled out of the water and the captain offered us rum. "No. Water," we had replied.

Then the other man sitting at the table introduced himself with a lifeless monotone, "Hi, I'm Bob."

"Nice to meet you, Bob," I replied.

It didn't take long to figure out who Bob was and his purpose for being part of the deposition process. I realized he had to be the attorney representing the insurance company or underwriter.

The main purpose of the deposition was to satisfy the insurance company's investigation of the claim prior to any payout for loss to the owner of the vessel. Certain "W" questions would need to be answered.

1. What does the owner have to gain by the loss of the vessel?
2. Where is the vessel?

The *Anhinga* was worth nearly a million dollars. The claim would require a large payout. So if the insurance company could prove the loss of the vessel had been a purposeful attempt to gain a large sum of money, they could deny the claim. It was easy to see why they might not exactly be on our side.

Of course, it was impossible to answer as to the exact location of the *Anhinga*. She was in thousands of pieces, no doubt strewn from the Florida Straits to somewhere off Maine by now. The engines and stingers were sure to be somewhere in the depths ninety miles outside of Key West. I thought about how much easier the process would have been if I had only kept the camera with the horrifying pictures of the wreckage that surrounded Eric and me.

I was trying my best to restrain my fear of making a mistake. The guy was a professional at making people say things he wanted them to say. I could only tell the truth as to what I had experienced during those many hours of struggle in the Gulf Stream. The deposition was indeed like the incident investigation lesson. The Old Dominion University professor assured us it was likely we'd be in a courtroom one day and, if so, we should directly answer any questions asked and then say absolutely nothing more.

The initial questions were rather simple in nature. I guess to build ease and to establish a baseline of trust. Then, the questions methodically progressed into reliving the nightmare. Now I understood why Captain Eric had come out of there with such a flood of emotions etched on his face.

During the few days between April 13 and the deposition, I had only talked about the intense fight to survive a couple times. In each of those discussions, I was able to back out of the story and shut it off before the emotions became too overwhelming. The reality was that I could never shut off the emotions before the tears started to flow. Reliving it was like getting in a fight with the sharks we had thankfully not had the pleasure of meeting.

The deposition experience continued to evolve. Bob was now asking all the lead-in questions to manipulate the answers toward his desired outcome. As much as I wanted to withdraw at certain points, his needling questions would not allow me to escape the terror. I so desperately wanted to escape the escalating torture. Everything about the manner of the attorney was nasty. I couldn't stop the tears. The evil man was crushing me to the core.

I was seeing a change in the position across the table. With each increasingly ruthless detail the attorney questioned, the more uneasy the adjuster for the insurance company became. Eventually, even the adjuster was looking at the attorney with disgust. He finally erupted on the heartless attorney with, "That is enough of those questions. Back off, now." I was an absolute emotional wreck. I was so extremely thankful for the adjuster's reaction to the unprofessional manner put on by the lawyer hired to represent the insurance company's interest.

I was able to finish the story in a less harassing environment, but the damage was done. I had been tormented into a place of psychological unrest and post-traumatic stress. I darted out the door when it was finally done. Captain Eric and I were both absolutely drained.

I desperately needed to escape to a place of peace. Where could I find enough peace to overcome the anxiety?

Captain Eric with his mates, present and past. Richard (right) was Eric's mate on the forty-three-foot Merritt's boat and the Jim Smith *Anhinga* boats from 1988 through 1996. Captain Eric (center) and me (left). Photo taken in 1998.

A cart full of fish made for happy charter customers and a nice tip at the end of the day. I was in my early to mid-twenties in this photo.

CHAPTER 16:

FIRST TIME BACK OUT ON THE MONSTER

Following the deposition, I had an intense feeling of being lost without a purpose. Captain Eric and I were exhausted after the torture test. From there, we parted ways as he headed back to Stuart. I needed some peace in my life, which was ironic given the amount of peace I should've had ahold of after being saved from such a dire situation. This is so typical of how we often respond after we have been blessed to make it through our struggles in life. God gets us through them, and then as soon as the seas get calm, we forget about what good things He has done for us. We forget about the horrible storm we've just been rescued from.

While in Florida, I seemed to be able to achieve peace through surfing or being on the boat. Working on the water falls into one of those job categories that becomes part of a person's being. Most people think of a waterman as someone who works on the water. But I was another group of watermen. I was made up of one whose job is going far out into the ocean to catch fish, one who harnesses the power of the sea to feel the rush of standing on a wave, and one who hunts fish in the water with a mask, fins, and a spear. I was one of many mates and captains to have this connection to the sea that flows through our veins.

I needed to find peace, and going surfing was the quickest way to achieve it. My first stop was Jupiter Beach Park to check the surf on the south side of Jupiter Inlet. I was so excited, I pulled into the first parking spot, jumped out of the Bronco, and ran to see what the Atlantic Ocean held in store for that day's therapy.

For a surfer, cresting the dunes is like waking up on Christmas morning. You may find the perfect gift or the undesirable pink bunny onesie from Aunt Clara. For me, on this day, it was the pink onesie. But this didn't deter my hope because I got back into the Bronco for an attempt to find better conditions four-hundred yards down the road at the inlet. There was no difference at the inlet, so I continued to check the secret spots where Scotty and I had been surfing all winter. I worked my way south toward Singer Island.

Pride was my inspiration to choose surfing as the first option. I was dreading the thought of walking down the dock at Sailfish Marina. Most of my friends were already in Mexico by now. Even the charter fleet was slightly smaller. Some had moved on to follow the sailfish in Mexico, while others were chasing marlin in the Bahamas. Regardless, I felt out of place walking down to the dock where I had no boat.

So often, pride holds us back from fulfilling what's planned for our lives. Pride is the cause of so much separation in our lives. Too often, pride causes separation between us and the things we love. All throughout the Bible, there are references to pride dividing. How many families have been ripped apart by pride? I'm convinced that if pride is removed from an argument between two people, the argument can be soothed into a discussion.

I almost allowed pride to keep me from walking down the charter dock that day at Sailfish Marina—a dock I had worked on for two seasons. It had only been about a week since I was fighting to survive in the Gulf Stream water. The tide was coming in, so the water flowing under the Sailfish Marina docks came from the Stream. I hoped I would not see anyone I knew. Especially someone who might want to hear my story.

With my head down, I took my first step onto the dock since the accident. It didn't take long to reach the *American Lady*. The door was open, so I knew Captain Joey must have been inside. Even though I held so much respect for him, I couldn't make the right turn on the finger pier to step aboard. I continued down the dock and passed my friend, walking down the center of the ten-foot-wide concert dock and trying not to look to either side.

I noticed a figure stepping off a boat and heading in my direction. My only escape would have been to jump in the blue Gulf Stream water that flows in Palm Beach Inlet of the flood tide. After considering this for a split second, I continued on to find it was Captain Dave. He was fortunate enough to run charter fishing trips on a really nice custom Carolina boat owned by his family.

The news of the *Anhinga* had traveled fast. Dave, captain of the *Passion*, seemed both shocked and thankful when we met eyes. We talked for a few minutes as I shared a couple of the details about the sinking, and he talked to me about how fishing had been. He explained how he had just booked a half-day charter for the next morning and how he was in a tough spot because he didn't have a mate for the trip. Then he popped the inevitable question. The question I was not prepared to answer.

"Can you work tomorrow?" the captain asked.

I didn't know what to say. The owner of the *Anhinga* was kind enough to continue my weekly salary for the duration I'd planned working on her. I didn't need the money, but then again, fishing had never been about the money. This question presented a true crossroads of life type of situation. Was I going to allow being lost at sea to prevent me from ever feeling the rush of wiring an eight-hundred-pound blue marlin again? Could I survive again?

"Yes, sir," my mouth replied, while my brain was wondering who'd given over command to the lips. Dave smiled. He explained he was leaving for the day to take care of some business and I could make myself at home on the boat. The key to being a good mate is being prepared. The time spent looking over the tackle and preparing rigs was the exact therapy I needed to overcome my pride and provide peace to my soul.

The next morning, I went through the regular routine of getting ready for a charter in Palm Beach. I started with breakfast at 6:00 a.m. to be on the boat by 6:30 a.m. On the way down to the charter dock, I stopped in the marina tackle shop to get sixty pounds of ice, fresh ballyhoo bait fish, and some extra number five stainless-wire for leaders, in case toothy critters were biting. Then, I stepped aboard the *Passion* with all of the items and stowed them away.

It was time to bring the fishing rods out to the cockpit and arrange them in the fighting chair used to tackle big fish. I had learned early on as a mate it is extremely important to make sure the cockpit is "styling and profiling" to make a good first impression with the charter customers as they come down the dock. That means making sure all the rods are lined up in the right spot. No one wants to see different sized rods and reels all jumbled together.

Dave arrived at the boat and watched for a moment before going into the engine room to perform his pre-trip checks. The goggle-eye live baits were doing well in the bait tank, and the ballyhoo were rigged and ready to go. Both bow lines, one of the spring lines, and the power cord were removed from the boat. Everything was ready to go. We watched the parking lot for the charter to show up.

The captain asked me another question: "Johnny. Are you ready for this?"

His question demonstrated how the industry is when it comes to caring about each other. Everything tackle- and fish-related thing on the boat screamed, "I am ready to go." Dave was concerned about the inside of me. I was so busy staying occupied with preparing that I hadn't even thought about the fact I was getting ready to go back out on the open ocean for the first time since the *Anhinga* sank. I simply nodded because I didn't have the words to describe how I was feeling.

The charter arrived, which broke the train of thought reflecting on my fear of returning to the very career that almost killed me. That morning was similar to when I was floating around out in the Gulf of Mexico in that I had a job to do. There was no time to think bad thoughts. The downtimes were rare, which helped to prevent the thoughts of doom. The wind was a perfect thirteen knots for flying the medium wind kite. Kite fishing might be one of the best presentations for a bait on the surface of the water because the fishing line from the rod and reel is held in the air so the fish can't see it. The method proved to be effective. That day, the fishing was steady and the charter had fun catching a sailfish and some mahi for dinner. This was my first time ever working for Dave, and I was very thankful for the opportunity. As an angler was cranking in a barracuda, the captain leaned over the rail and said it's time to reel everything in. Time flies when having fun, and it was time to head back to the dock.

The boat was turned to the west as the fishing gear was organized for the run home. I briefly chatted with the charter before heading up to the bridge. I was at peace when climbing the ladder, feeling like this was what I was made to do. Clearly, I had to brush off the dust of struggle and climb back on the horse—or boat, in my case. When I got up on the bridge, I stood next to Dave with enthusiasm. That is, until I looked beyond the bow deck to see what was in front of us.

A mass of dark-billowing clouds was evolving directly before us along the coast, as far as we could see in both directions. The white condominiums and hotels were such a contrast to the mixture of dark blues, purples, grays, and blacks of the enormous squall that was about to advance on the turquoise-blue ocean. Dave looked with concern as I quickly dropped down the ladder to tell the charter to get inside and stay in the salon.

Upon returning to the bridge to standby for orders, all I could think was, *"Here we go again. Why did I do this so soon?"* Although I was scared, we were only a mile and a half off the beach. I could swim that far.

The wall of wind eventually hit us as the ocean's surface went flat and white from the intense winds. Most Carolina-built boats have a sharp entry at the bow that extends up and out to where the hull at the upper bow flattens horizontally. This design is called "Carolina Flare," as it's unique to these boats to help cut through the rough southwesterly winds of the mid-Atlantic.

The boat's bow pointed directly into the wind. The wind was screaming in the rigging and was so strong it was able to catch the flare like a sail. I could feel the wind lifting on the bow of the boat. The lightning was coming down all around us. The rain cut visibility down to less than fifty yards. To our dismay, one of the side curtains blew out. Next, one of the six-foot seat cushions on the bridge lifted and took off, flying from the bridge into the mess of angry waves.

As quick as the storm came in, it was gone, heading offshore toward the Bahamas. The whole event lasted less than ten minutes but felt as if it had stopped time. Captain Dave gave me a look once it was all over, and we both just laughed. Everything was good.

This was my last trip out of Palm Beach for the 1998 season. The brand-new Fifty Viking Yacht had been delivered from the factory in New Jersey to Bluewater Yacht Sales in Hampton. Captain Steve was ready for me to get to work helping him get her rigged up for the upcoming fishing season.

To top it off, my buddy Jimbo wanted to see me for a final request before I headed home. We had been friends since junior high and were both mates working on boats at the same marinas. All winter, he had been encouraging me to ask his sister out. I overcame my fear and called to see if she would like to go on a date. She said "yes." I couldn't pack up the gear at my aunt's house and head north to Virginia fast enough. God always has a way of putting people in our life at just the right time.

PART 2:

THE ANATOMY OF A MIRACLE

CHAPTER 17:

THE SCIENCE

Over the years, there have been a number of stories written by or about people who have claimed to have met God. I do not and will not deny what they claim to be true. They were there in the moment, and I was not. The unique thing about the story of the *Anhinga* is that it defies science and probabilities of rescue.

In the next few sections, my goal is to bring you a little closer to understanding some of the mysteries of the sea and why I consider it nothing short of a miracle that we were rescued. I also want to bring you some understanding of the responsibility associated with operating one of these multi-million-dollar fishing machines.

WARM WATER HYPOTHERMIA

Throughout the years following the accident, I have struggled to understand the details of how hypothermia affects the body in seventy-nine-degree water. My understanding of this potentially deadly medical condition was better than average. As a safety professional with a concentration in the area of industrial hygiene, I am required to know how physical hazards adversely affect a worker's body. Thermal exposure is one of those physical hazards. Most of my training and experience was geared toward preventing heat stress-related illness. Cold stress is not as big of a concern living in coastal Virginia where we may see snow two or three times a year. An inch of snow actually sticking to the ground is enough to close almost everything down in Hampton Roads.

I have no formal training specialized in the thermal physiological effects of prolonged exposure in the water. Most of what I have known is from my experience as a surfer and occasional freediving. I understood my body was about ninety-eight degrees, and the water was seventy-nine degrees, so eventually my core temperature would be dropping.

The first moment of deeper understanding came when a high school friend invited me to speak to a group of teenagers at the church where he's the youth pastor. Prior to speaking, he informed me that some of the teens in the group were dealing with issues unique to kids who have a father who is a US Military Special Operator. My heart sank for the struggles these teens were dealing with.

While sharing the story, it was put on my heart to go into detail about my attempt to commit suicide. My initial statement in that part of the story was, "I've never fully understood how Captain Eric and I were affected by hypothermia while immersed in seventy-nine-degree water."

All of a sudden, one of the youth group leaders at the back right of the room stood up and said, "Specific gravity."

What he said made sense. According to Dictionary.com, specific gravity is "the ratio of any substance to the density of some other substance taken as a standard, water being the standard for liquids and solids." The Gulf Stream runs through the tropics prior to coming up and traveling through the Gulf of Mexico. We float easier in tropical water because the level of salt is higher; therefore, the water is denser than seawater in the northern Atlantic.

This leader, who was also the father of one of the teens, is a retired Navy SEAL. He was trained with the knowledge that the specific gravity of the Caribbean water is 1.023 kg/m3 to 1.026 kg/m3, and the male human body is about 0.98 kg/m3. He explained the seawater I was saturated in was pulling the moisture out of my body to get closer to equilibrium.

SEALs and other Navy divers prepare for missions that require extended exposure in salt water by hydrating in advance to compensate for the water their cells will lose due to specific gravity. Captain Eric and I had no idea the very seawater that provided for and sustained us as fishermen was killing us by extracting the water from our bodies.

Long after the fact, I knew there was still something missing in terms of fully understanding hypothermia. In God's true and consistent faithfulness, He provided me with the right time to write this part of the book. I received a phone call from a neighbor who needed help building a fence. It was his kid's first year in the Virginia Beach 4-H Livestock Club, and he needed someone with a truck to pick up supplies for the goat pen.

I knew my neighbor was a diver in the Navy, but I wasn't exactly sure about what type of diver he was. He knew a little bit about my story of being lost at sea. We had an opportunity to talk for the hour trip to and from the Tractor Supply store. It was the first time I had ever talked to someone who could closely relate to the experience of floating in the deep blue sea for an extended period of time.

My friend told me about how in the middle of the open ocean, his team would deploy from naval vessels and be left there for three or four hours. He said the big difference was "we had strobes and locating beacons, and we knew the vessel was coming back to get us." They tried not to look down into the water. As divers, they had seen the man-eaters that swim below in the very same area the *Anhinga* sank. Occasionally, one of the specialists would make a joke about seeing something below. He said the team didn't think the sick joke was very funny. They were all a little terrified.

He understood the struggle of what it was like to keep from ingesting seawater when talking or breathing. He understood the loneliness, the absence of security, the mighty roar of the sea during a storm, and the sting of the spray blowing in his face. He also understood the hypothermia.

They would prepare for the exposure by getting a good night's sleep prior to the mission or training exercise. He stressed how important that was to fending off hypothermia. I'd never known rest was a factor. I'd failed to get a good night's sleep by staying up too late to fill an addiction for catching tarpon. The fish almost immediately take to the sky—jumping when they are hooked—which make them hard to land in order to release them. I would have had a lot more than three hours of sleep if I'd followed the marina's no tarpon fishing rules.

While waiting for the Navy vessel to return, the team would huddle in a circle to keep the currents from pulling them apart. He has experienced the initial symptoms of hypothermia while in eighty-degree water within three and four hours of being deployed. Keep in mind, this happened to him while wearing a wetsuit with neoprene that is three-millimeters thick.

I desperately needed understanding about the hypothermia to bring a sense of closure to that portion of my life. The neighbor's testimony and the *US Navy Diving Manual* provided the final peace of assurance I needed in writing this part. According to the manual, immersion hypothermia occurs when the difference between the body and water temperature is large enough to cause the body to lose more heat than it can metabolically create. The manual also states, "A water temperature of approximately 91°F (33°C) is required to keep an unprotected, resting man at a stable temperature." Acclimatization and experience were two factors working in my favor due to all the hours spent surfing, swimming, and free diving prior to the encounter with the rogue wave.

THE 1997 EL NIÑO

High seas weather forecasting in 1998 pales in comparison to our current technologies. Today's marine electronics allow a captain to obtain the latest forecast by simply moving the cursor over a desired location on an electronic nautical chart and clicking enter. The current forecast for the area is then downloaded from a satellite. Current capabilities allow us to overlay real-time weather data recorded by the vessel's instrumentation with real-time satellite data. The vessel's radar and XM/Sirius Weather radars can be combined on one screen to display current conditions with amazing accuracy. We can also determine the safest point to punch through an approaching squall based on the concentration of lightning strike icons on the satellite radar.

In 1998, the best option for maritime forecast was through the National Oceanic and Atmospheric Administration (NOAA) and Weather Routers forecasting service. Captain Eric had obtained a high-seas forecast for the lower Gulf of Mexico and listened to the NOAA Marine Forecast for the region prior to our departure from Key West on the morning of April 13, 1998. According to the forecast, we had a window to safely make our crossing from Key West, Florida, to Isla Mujeres, Mexico. We had no way of knowing what the Pacific Ocean was going to throw at us while ninety miles out into the Gulf of Mexico.

A unique weather event was also occurring in the Pacific Ocean during 1997 and 1998: El Niño. According to scientists, the El Niño weather pattern of late 1997 was the strongest ever recorded. The scenario allowed for warmer than normal sea surface temperatures to exist in the eastern Pacific Ocean from southern California down into South America. This is why I was able to surf the Trestles point break wearing a light spring-suit type of wetsuit.

A climatologist who is part of the Center for Oceanic Atmospheric Prediction Studies presented information on how El Niño could have impacted the weather around the world. In one of the slides, he showed how a storm could develop in the Pacific and travel easterly directly over where Captain Eric and I were lost at sea. The rapidly developed storm we had to endure while fighting for our lives may have developed because of El Niño. It was active on April 13, 1998. Of course, we'll never know whether this was truly the case or not, but it gave me the solace of a possible explanation.

It is a scientific fact that tequila does not grow on trees, but we sure had fun hanging the bottles. Puerto Aventuras, Mexico, 1997 on Park Avenue dock

First Place Tournament Win—Virginia Beach Red, White & Blue Marlin Tournament. Norm Isaacs with ESPN is interviewing Captain Jimmy and I aboard the *Sniper*. Captain Jimmy (left), me (center), and Captain Norm Isaacs (right).

CHAPTER 18:

MAJOR MOTION ON THE SEA

Writing this book was therapeutic in some ways. I received the closure in understanding the rogue wave that destroyed the *Anhinga*. I'd struggled with the science behind the wave before. It did not fit into the box of possible waves and wave patterns I knew of. The other struggle was and continues to be the psychological aspect of what happened out there while lost at sea. The likely surprise of some, think the sight, sound, and feeling of the monstrous wave is slightly more traumatic than my attempted suicide. It seems there is a form of post-traumatic stress disorder (PTSD) that affects mariners who have come into contact with rogue waves.

When I was asked about what the wave looked like, I always had a reservation of doubt in describing it because I didn't understand it. Eric and I talked a lot about what the wave looked like. There was one thing for certain: In all my days of fishing, I had never seen anything even close to resembling the rogue wave that sank the *Anhinga*. To have a wave large enough for the fifty-six-foot *Anhinga* to enter and fall at a sharp angle with bow down within the overall two- to three-foot sea state is a freak occurrence.

Unlike in *The Perfect Storm* movie, there was not a visible vertical wall in front of us. I often refer to the rogue wave as a hole that the *Anhinga* fell into because of the sensation of falling that overcame me. All focus was centered on the bow, and everything else was part of my peripheral vision. I have no idea how far the wave extended in either direction to our side. I do know it was a massive and powerful force of water that would have likely sunk any boat.

I struggled because, as I've mentioned, the monster that I saw didn't fit into the wave patterns I had learned in school or at the wave exhibit in the Virginia Marine Science Museum. I gained peace in the process of researching information about rogue waves for this book. Prior to the middle of the 1990s, there was relatively little information.

According to the *BBC2 Horizon-Freak Wave* documentary, the Draupner oil platform was struck by a rogue wave on January 1, 1995, at about 3:20 p.m. The instrumentation of the rig in the North Sea was able to read the wave as it passed. It was a nearly thirty-meter wave in a twelve-meter average sea state. This wave shocked the world and changed everything.

The use of satellites was employed to scan the surface of the ocean to better determine the frequency of these freak wave events. The data revealed these events occurred a lot more often than what was previously determined to be a one in ten-thousand year event. The linear model that has been used in vessel design for years may not work for the frequency and shape of this monster that is traveling the seas looking for a vessel to devour. The identity of the ancient sea monster had been discovered. The loss of the vessel could not be totally blamed on structural faults or operator error/human factor.

Any mariner who has faced the beast and lived through it is changed forever. Documented firsthand accounts of rogue waves are relatively rare. The freak waves can take a large ship and stretch between the crests or tops of waves, which causes the middle of the ship to hang in the opening of the trough. The hanging weight of the midsection then collapses. Typically, in this case, there is no one left to tell the story. The result is absolute terror and tragedy.

As I watched various documentaries about rogue waves in preparing to write this testimony, I realized that many of the crew members interviewed had a similar look. The terror is enough to put the toughest captains in tears. The rogue wave is a force of nature like nothing else. What I heard in their voices and saw in their eyes was the same terror I had felt inside for so many years. Some form of PTSD certainly plagues mariners who have seen the monster.

So much of the information needed to write this portion of the book has come at the perfect time to help you, too, understand what happened that day on April 13, 1998. Ron is a friend and a coworker. He and I have talked a lot about family over the years. We knew how each other was raised and where. I knew Ron was a marine, his father was a Vietnam veteran serving in the Navy, and his grandfather was a solider in World War II. Ron lived with his grandparents for a while growing up while his mother traveled with his father as he worked on various construction projects. He had also mentioned how his grandparents loved each other very much, but they didn't sleep together.

He and his grandfather shared war stories for the first and only time when Ron returned home after fighting in Kosovo.

He knew his grandfather suffered from PTSD, but he was not sure of the source. Was it from the horrors of combat in WWII? Or was it from the pain of his' eldest son being killed in action at the onset of the war in Vietnam? Ron soon learned the root of his grandfather's PTSD, which was the reason his grandparents didn't sleep in the same bed at night.

Near the end of WWII, his grandfather was on *Destroyer, USS-Wiltsie* in the Pacific Fleet in the South China Sea. They were part of a group of ships that were out at sea when a typhoon catastrophically struck the fleet. The waves were enormous, and the fleet was in peril. During the night, the depth charges that were stowed on the bow deck broke free from the storage. The loose charges presented an immediate risk to the ship. Ron's grandfather and his best friend were given orders to go out in the dark with their flashlights to secure the charges.

The fate of the ship rested on the orders being carried out. With bow rising and falling, the waves would wash over the decks. The ship took on an incredibly large wave while the two men were executing their task. Ron's grandfather looked over to only find a flashlight on deck. His best friend had been washed overboard into the sea without hope of rescue. When the storm passed, the ship had to make port to repair storm damage. A number of sailors and soldiers went AWOL, as the storm scared them so bad they chose to never set foot on a ship again. His grandfather's PTSD was neither from battle nor his son being killed in action; it was from his experience with the fury of the sea.

There is little information documenting the event that rocked Ron's grandfather. I feel this is a great example of the power of the horror a destructive wave holds. While writing this book, I shared the story of the *Anhinga* with a men's fellowship group in Suffolk, Virginia. Following the speech, two gentlemen approached to inform me of another person they knew of whose life was wrecked by the same storm that affected Ron's grandfather.

The *Anhinga* was a well-built and structurally sound vessel. Jim Smith was known for using state-of-the-art materials and techniques to build boats that were stronger so they could go faster. One thing I learned following the accident was that safety is a priority to the builders of production and custom sportfishing yachts.

Some of the most well-known boat builders and designers in the industry have asked to hear the story of the *Anhinga*. Some of those builders, designers, and fabricators are Omie Tillet of Sportsman boats, Bill and Pat Healey of Viking Yachts, John Vance of Jim Smith boats, Earle Hall of Bluewater Yacht Sales, Paul Mann, John Bayliss, Paul Spencer, Bobby Crowait, Nelva Capps, Billy Maxwell, Wayne Umphlett, Dominick LaCombe, Merritt, Rybovich, and many others. They all had the same reason for wanting to hear the story, and they all had similar looks on their faces; they all care deeply about their customers.

The look was one of discernment as they tried to figure out what had gone wrong or failed. The fact is, even the plans designed by the best marine architect in the world with their specified materials would have been challenged. The force of the wave that took out the *Anhinga* was too powerful, and the vessel would have been lost in any case. The builders and designers want to meet the desires of their customers, but mostly, they want their customers, families, friends, and crews to be safe. These craftsmen are proud of the amazing yachts they build. Each boat is unique. I have been a part of the sports fishing industry for over thirty years. One thing

I have learned is that craftsmen are not too proud to ask for help when it comes to continuously improving the safety of their builds.

I had the opportunity to run one of the first Viking 60s to be manufactured. The owner had a great eye for detail, so the brand-new *Episode* would be in Bluewater's service yard for a couple months undergoing customization. There was another boat in the yard with a tuna tower that was too tall to fit under the Rudee Inlet Bridge. The aluminum structure of sunshade at the very top of the tower would need to be cut and hinged to drop back and provide clearance to pass under.

This is not typically a big deal, but this one had a very heavy satellite dish on top of the sunshade. Earle Hall designed a system with a winch and series of pulleys to lower and raise the top. His fabricators made and installed the system. Since Earle just so happened to have a captain hanging around on his boat yard, who is also a safety engineer, he asked me to have a look at the system. It was robust. That's an old term Ford and UAW Safety Team members used for, "It's stronger than it needs to be," which is a good thing. The only recommendation I could find was the standard safety go-to: "Perform regular inspection of the cable and connections." The tower project could hardly compare to the *Knot Done Yet* project where Bluewater provided a quadriplegic the ability to safely pursue his passion of fishing.

Building custom sportfishing yachts is a true art. Each builder has their own signatures designed into the shape or the lines of the boat. The personal touch might be the engine room vent, sheer-line, flybridge, or deck turn-down, or maybe the stem. Custom Carolina boats can be the most difficult to distinguish between brands because many of the lines are similar and there are several builders stretched out between Nags Head and Morehead City, North Carolina.

Paul Mann is one of those builders whose signature can be found at the rear of his salon window line. His signature is also in the safety of his boats. Building things safer costs more money, but for Paul, it's worth a cut into profit to build collision and water-tight bulkheads throughout his boats. He is one of those charter boat captains turned yacht builder. The boats used to be simple boats with interiors a little bit nicer than a school bus with a refrigerator. Now they are yachty with gorgeous plush interiors made from the rarest cuts of wood. Paul is proud of the work produced by his talented craftsmen. He is the kind of man who would give the shirt off his back to a child or person in need. My friend has an edge of zeal, which is translated into the personality of his boats.

When he talks about the safety of the custom boats he builds, it's all heartfelt true humbleness. I recently asked him about his commitment to building a safe vessel.

"It hits deep. People are putting their lives on the line to go out there on the ocean on something I built," Paul Mann replied.

Hull design is another factor that can vary based on sea state and sea direction. Jim Smith boats are known for having an amazing ride in a following sea. Custom Carolina boats are great head sea boats because of their sharp entry in the bow rising up to a flared section to shed the water. The flared bow is not just made to look pretty, it's shaped to meet the unique conditions of the Outer Banks and Mid-Atlantic. Great head sea boats are needed due to the afternoon southwest winds creating three- to four-foot waves that the point of the bow must cut through to get back home.

Larger boats will knock down the seas by their mass. Last summer, I ran the sixty-six Viking, *Desperado*. She had over one hundred thousand pounds of displacement to break a nineteen-foot-wide path through the waves. I was honored to be able to clear the way for some of my past captains who invested so much in my training. Comfort was also provided in knowing the *Desperado* had a strong keel. When Viking Yacht builds their boats, they fill the void of the keel section with a mixture of resin and pebbles, making it like concrete.

One November night, I had just finished cleaning the teak in preparing the boat to go to Florida for the winter when Joe, Bev, and Emmy came out of the house in pajamas to hang out on the boat. I had been their captain all summer, but I had never shared the whole story of the *Anhinga* with them until that night. After we shed some tears, Bev said the thing I had heard so many times before: "You have to write a book about your testimony." For some reason, this night the Holy Spirit put a conviction on my heart stronger than ever before about writing this story to share with others.

Uniquely, back in the early nineties, I was the mate for Joe's parents on their fifty-five-foot Gwaltney Custom Carolina boat, *No Problem*.

I remember his father's famous words of wisdom: "Son, you can marry more money in five minutes than you can make in a lifetime. Don't do what I did. I went to West Virginia and married the poorest woman I could find, and I've been working my butt off ever since." He laughed with a lovingly peaceful laugh. It warms my heart every time his son laughs. He has the same laugh as his father who is now most certainly in Heaven with the wife he loved so much. His wealth was not in money in the bank, investments, or property. His wealth was in his love for the Lord, his wife, and his family. Admittedly, though, it does take a bit of wealth to own and care for these high-performance fishing machines.

Sportfishing boats are vessels with a very specific purpose to their design. They are working fishing boats with high, pointy bows to cut through the choppy seas and a low, square stern for anglers and mates to work closer to the water level catching and hauling in fish. As well-built as these boats are, they have their limits against the power of the oceans. I will never forget what it looked like as the *Anhinga* fell down the face of that rogue wave.

The experience I gained over the years by working as a mate prepared me to respond when the *Anhinga* was struck by the rogue wave, as well as an incident that occurred in 2000. I was the mate on the *Sniper* during an early, pitch-black December morning. The *Sniper* was struck against what was likely a submarine off the coast of Virginia. The black object had no lights and no radar signature. Captain Jimmy went to action with the lifesaving Mayday call to the US Coast Guard. Our charter passengers were rescued, and the *Sniper* was saved by the collision bulkhead forward of the engine room. Paul Mann had installed this collision bulkhead even though it was not required at the time he built the vessel. The official report said the *Sniper* struck a sea container, but there were black scuff marks at the waterline and high above at the bow deck. I have never seen a black sea container or Conex box.

These events had prepared me for the day I became a captain in 2001.

Caipirinhas at the Papaya Republic Restaurant "Monkey Bar," Puerto Aventuras, Mexico. Me (left), Rob, April, and Captain Sean (right).

CHAPTER 19:

CONTANGO AND EPISODES OF A CAPTAIN

Safety of the vessel and everyone onboard is the primary responsibility of any captain. The proper response when dangerous situations arise is critical. The largest part of knowing how to respond comes from spending time out on the water and lessons learned from past experiences. Therefore, the US Coast Guard (USCG) requires service time in addition to the successful completion of the appropriate mariner's course and exam. I was a mate for about fifteen years before I decided to get my captain's license. I figured driving the boat was the easy part. The hard part was finding and catching the fish. I needed to be confident that I had gained experience prior to stepping up to the bridge. I owed it to the customers who pinched pennies and did without all year long so they could afford to go on an offshore charter fishing once a year. If I did not have the knowledge and skill to go out there and perform to my best ability, I was just robbing them of the money they'd worked so hard for.

I started working on head boats, which fall under a law that requires periodic Coast Guard inspections on vessels for hire that carry seven or more passengers. There were also vessel design and safety gear requirements to maintain compliance as a USGC inspected vessel. Eventually, I moved on to work on the *High Hope*, which is a custom Carolina-built sportfish with the rare classification of being an inspected vessel. I feel the annual duties required to prepare and participate in the annual hands-on compliance inspections performed by the USCG made me more aware and serious about the safety requirements. Once again, the Lord tends to prepare your path.

The first charter I ever ran was on a Paul Mann boat called the *Sniper*. I knew the boat fairly well after working as the mate for Jimmy, the owner and operator, for a couple years. As we cleared the tip of the rock jetties, a tropical storm that was hundreds of miles away was sending large southeast ground swells that were breaking around Rudee Inlet as they approached. All of a sudden, both motors shut off. The boat was adrift on a path that would take it past the tip of the rock jetties, into the breakers, and then onto the beach.

There was a plan for Jimmy to run the *Sniper* 620 miles to Bermuda the next day. It was not looking good. After a quick system reset, the motors would not start. A quick decision was made to abort getting the motors started, and the order was given to deploy the anchor. My good friend, James, was the mate. He quickly went into action. He set the anchor on the first try, and we tied off just shy of the waves breaking on the sandbar off the beach. Captain Steve on the *Backlash* had just pulled out of his slip at the Virginia Beach Fishing Center prior to standing by to assist. After some troubleshooting, we discovered the main twenty-four-volt electrical breaker failed. I was able to get it to make contact again and fire up the motors. We made our way back to the boat slip where

Tom, an electrician with the Bluewater Yachts Service team, was standing by to make whatever repairs were necessary. He fixed the *Sniper*. James and I headed back out with the charter and had a great day of white marlin and mahi fishing. Teamwork and experience saved the *Sniper* that day.

Years later, I would have one of my biggest scares while running a fifty-six-foot Viking Yacht called the *Episode*. Jack, my toddler son, was the only one on the boat with me, which made it extremely scary. There should always be another able seaman onboard when underway with these multimillion-dollar yachts. I was moving the boats from Ricky and Julianne's house back to our slip at Fisherman's Wharf in Rudee Inlet. There was a flat-bottomed dinner-cruise boat directly in front of me through a relatively narrow channel in the Lynnhaven waterway. I laid the outriggers out to a lower and spread-out position so the *Episode* would fit through the bridge. The outgoing tidal water was pushing both vessels toward the bridge as we traveled parallel to it.

Out of nowhere, both boats were struck in the side by a near hurricane force gust of wind from a rapidly developed squall. The gust hit her port side so hard it blew the outrigger pole up, and it slammed into the overhead latch welded to the flybridge tower structure. "Bang," the whole bridge vibrated as Jack was still sound asleep on the front bench. The wind and the outgoing tide were both in the same direction pushing both boats broadside into the Lesner Bridge. The City of Virginia Beach used to have an enormous sign with a grim reaper saying "IT'S A BEAUTIFUL PLACE TO DROWN!" on it and the astonishing number of people who had died in the very spot we were drifting toward.

Based on experience with the *Episode*'s power and handling characteristics, I was able to quickly use the pair of

1,500-horsepower of each of the motors to maneuver her to safety. The most important thing to do was provide the less responsive cruise boat the room it needed to keep clear of the grim reaper. The captain of the cruise boat did a great job. This was another example of how experience saved the day. The other half of my crew was still asleep.

Oregon Inlet and Hatteras Inlet are known as two of the most dangerous inlets on the East Coast due to the ever-shifting channel, which is narrow and shallow. But it is the gauntlet of breaking waves over an extensive stretch of bars or shoals that wreaks havoc on a captain's nerves as he passes through. The inlets are so dangerous, the charts are blank and instead give advice to seek local knowledge. I experienced firsthand the risks associated with Hatteras Inlet's Shoals during my years at the helm of the *Contango*. It happened during the 2019 Hatteras Marlin Club Blue Marlin Tournament.

The morning started with the regular pre-trip safety inspection on the sixty-foot Viking with all visible mechanical and electronic systems good. After breakfast, Kevin, the mate, casted off the lines, and we happened to be the lead boat in a pack of about ten state-of-the-art sportfishing machines. While on the point position, we carried the line through ten miles of the twisting path leading through the Pamlico Sound to Hatteras Inlet. In many areas, the channel was shallow and narrow. We try to keep the boat running up high on a plane while running through shallow water because it reduces the depth needed to make passage. I think the second boat in a line has the best spot. The first boat will be the first to make impact if the channel has shifted, and boats toward the back of the line are at a great risk of running aground because the boats in front of them have pushed considerable amounts of water out of the channel.

I was running her at a low cruise of twenty-seven knots when we came off the second to last turn before heading out the inlet and across the bar. There was an outgoing tide pushing us toward what was a long sandbar directly off the starboard side. Our wake was breaking on the bar as we approached the final right-hand turn to exit the inlet. I performed a quick wiggle of the steering wheel just prior to the turn, but there was no response in the rudders. I quickly glanced up to see if the autopilot had inadvertently turned on. It had not, and we were on the channel-buoy marking the turn. Directly in front of us was a long, shallow sandbar running perpendicular to us.

Boats do not have brakes. I quickly pulled the throttle levels back to neutral on the pair of 1,900-horsepower Caterpillars. The engine's computer determined the rapid reduction in power was an unexpected communication fault, and both engines shut down as the *Contango* was still heading toward the bar. She would not directly restart, so I quickly shut down the main power to each engine to reset the engine's computers.

A quick wave of the arm signaled the boat following to go around to get them out of the danger zone as the current was pushing them toward the parallel sandbar. At low tide, much of the sand bar was exposed. There was no time for repair while drifting toward the bar and broadside out toward the shoals. Her two rudders were turned hard over as far as they could go, making the boat want to turn to her port, or left. I was able to use the throttles to steer. The port engine was throttled up, and I feathered the right engine in and out of gear. We made it across the shoals into safe waters. My nerves were shot and my blood pressure was probably higher than the gauge at the doctor's office could possibly read. The weight was lifted once the *Contango* was in safe waters.

The owner, an experienced boat handler, was by my side the whole time. With an astonished expression, he looked me dead in my eyes and said, "If I was at the wheel, I would have just lost my boat. Thank you."

"Boss, I was a little worried myself that I was going to lose her or someone would get hurt," I replied.

In that moment, an unbreakable bond of trust was sealed between Gary and me.

I yelled for Kevin to open the hatches to the lazarette. The drive system for the rudder is located in this compartment below the cockpit deck near the back of the boat. I shot down the ladder and poked my head in for an assessment of the mechanical failure that happened in nine feet of water. The seven-eighths-inch diameter steel bolt that attaches the steering arm to the rudder guide bar had sheered apart. Knowing we did not have a bolt that big in spare parts, I went into the engine room to rob one from something we didn't need.

The *Shenandoah*, a beautiful sixty-one-foot Spencer Yacht, circled back around to check on us. Captain Alan searched his spare parts and found one that would work to save our day. With the temporary fix installed, we ran back to the Hatteras Marlin Club. The boss ran to the hardware store and bought a seven-eighths-inch grade-eight bolt. My friend, Chip, passed down the necessary tools as I installed the new bolt. Within forty minutes, we were back underway.

There is nothing uniquely spectacular about these stories. Many captains managed situations much more serious than these. A captain's leadership role starts with the safety of his crew, his passengers, and the vessel. From there, the job requires whatever occupation is necessary to maintain the course: mechanic, doctor, law enforcement, and psychologist at times. The true nature of the position shines when someone is in trouble. No one is left in peril on the sea.

One fact I have learned over the years is that there is one admiral who reigns supreme over all others. He has helped me to get out of more rough seas in life than any other. Boats can always be replaced, but the lives of those onboard cannot.

My first trip as charter boat captain with James (right) as the mate aboard the *Sniper*, a fifty-eight-foot Paul Mann Custom Boat (July 2001). James and I still fish together.

Crew of the *Episode* after a great day of marlin fishing. Mate Drew (left) and Captain Johnny (right).

PART 3:

TELLING THE STORY AND CHANGING LIVES

CHAPTER 20:

POLICE, SEALS, AND A SNIPER— LIFE IS PRECIOUS

This book started with a letter written to you from a park across from the SEAL Heritage Center. There's something unique about what is now called SEAL Park. As a very young boy in the late '70s and early '80s, I would play there with my best friend. He lived next door, and we spent many days fishing together in their pond or wherever our fathers would take us. When I was ten years old, his parents took us to this park for annual SEAL Team reunions. His father was a lieutenant commander with the SEALs, and I can't help but think he may have been present the day the prayer in the author's note was given.

My best friend and I were inseparable. We went to many other functions together such as Capability Demonstrations on base, reenactments at the Yorktown Battlefield, and boat parades at Harborfest in Norfolk. One of the best parts was the benefits of VIP status due to his father's position in the Navy. Sometimes we would ride on the bus with the warriors and spend time with their families. At this young age, I recognized two things about them. The SEALs were a very tight brotherhood; they were all like best friends. The other was that something was different about their families. Although I couldn't see it in my neighbor's family, I did sense some sort of pain in many of the others. Maybe my best friend's father received his peace through the Lord.

As with many military families, our friendship became a casualty of a transfer. His father was stationed in the Pentagon where he would achieve the rank of captain. I have never forgotten them and my love for fishing that was cultivated through them. For so many, the love of fishing, hunting, golfing, or any other hobby is planted by a father's love. A seed was planted that grew into a career all because of the investment of time provided by my father and my best friend's father.

In the late '80s, a large group of SEALs and their families had chartered the head boat I was working on for a day of deep-sea fishing. While untangling fishing lines and baiting hooks, I detected feeling the same sense I had as a child as I watched the interaction between the warriors and their families. There were senses of both deep love and deep pain. I cannot discuss the details, but in 2017, it became clear. I was able to witness how the whole family's suffering was directly related to sacrifices made by the special operator who was protecting freedom.

There have been multiple situations, whether at a friend's house or at some other sort of function, where I have been asked to share the story of the *Anhinga*. I am always amazed by the mutual connection made based on the understanding of what it feels like to be in the ocean alone and afraid. In the process of writing this, I realized that each time one of these elite warriors have asked to hear the story, it has never happened in the presence of their family. Maybe one reason is because they don't want their wives and children to know what it is like when they become part of the food chain. They also want to protect their loved ones from knowing the evils they have witnessed to exist in this world. I think sometimes the very scars they try to keep within to protect their families may end up hurting the family. These warriors are not the only group who see evil and hardship on a regular basis.

One day, I was driving home from work when I received a call from a friend who was in tears out of love for his brothers and sisters in law enforcement. He had worked several rolls in the Virginia Beach Police Department over the decades. One of those positions was a violent crimes detective where he saw how horrible evil can truly be. He also played a role in the team that responded to the City of Virginia Beach Municipal Center, Building Number Two mass shooting when a disgruntled municipal employee killed twelve people.

The friend who called had heard the story of the *Anhinga*. He said this about the story: "The first time I heard the story I was speechless. There were no words to match the emotions I was feeling. It is hard to imagine how someone could survive in such terrible conditions." After hearing the story, he knew God was real. I knew others needed to hear the story to give them hope in dealing with the job. They needed encouragement to keep fighting through the psychological and physical stress.

The emotions of thirty years of witnessing evil had built up, and the skeletons could no longer be confined to the closets they had been locked away in for so many years. The officers needed some sort of outreach where they could get out in the woods or sit around a campfire in a small group to speak the emotions that have been bottled up inside for decades. Our family was blessed to have a farm in the middle of the woods in Goochland County, Virginia. It was the perfect place to provide an atmosphere for the officers to talk openly.

Over the weekend, we cut firewood, walked through the woods, did some shooting, and stayed up late around a campfire talking. The setting was a place where it was alright for men to talk and shed tears. My friend had informed me of some startling statistics. Recent studies indicate that law enforcement officers and other first responders are exposed to traumatic events, which leads to PTSD. According to the international Public Safety Association, on average, police officers experience 188 critical incidents during their career. The average citizen will experience a couple events in a lifetime.

Two amazing things happened on that weekend on the farm. The first was that a sniper helped me to get a great grouping on long-range shots. The other, and most important thing, was realizing that dealing with evil to protect the rest of society often rips apart the lives of law enforcement and service members emotionally and physically. My friend had asked me to share the story of the *Anhinga* while we were sitting at the campfire, so I did. But there was a more important story that needed to be told. They needed to know the story of evil coming into this world for the first time.

Our soldiers, police officers, and first responders are sent into battle unprepared. I'm not talking about bulletproof vests and fully-automatic weapons. I'm talking about what really matters. They are not trained on who their enemy is.

> *Finally, be strong in the Lord and in His mighty power. Put on the full armor of God, so that you can take your stand against the devil's schemes. For our struggle is not against flesh and blood, but against the rulers, against the authorities, against the powers of this dark world and against the spiritual forces of evil in the heavenly realms (Ephesians 6 10-12 NIV).*

One of the officers siting around the campfire that night in Goochland was a marine sniper. He said this about the story of the *Anhinga*: "Special operators receive a lot of training about how to survive in dangerous situations, and there is a plan with backups standing by for extraction. You didn't have the training, and no one was coming to get you. That is why people like me and SEALs would feel like your story is such a bigger risk. Your will to survive is the hallmark of the human spirit. God whispered to you, and you didn't go under to kill yourself. You listened to what He told you and you went." The officer expressed how much admiration he has for the normal person who runs to the fight.

Many of the police officers in the United States and across the world see evil almost every day while on the job. As I listened to the police officers share their stories around the campfire, I knew of the evil they described. It was the definition of who Satan is. He is an evil liar that is out to destroy, kill, and divide.

The brave soldiers of the free world may not see evil daily, but they see horrors that occur in societies that reject Jesus. My friend, who was a US marine at the tip of the spear during the war in Kosovo, once described breaching a door to discover a room that was used for torture. He could sense the presence of evil in the empty chamber.

Another friend grew up watching his mother pray and go to church, but he went into combat not personally knowing Jesus. In Afghanistan as a US Navy SEAL, he saw things the Taliban had done to people that couldn't be described. "Johnny, I saw things they did to people that were so evil, we couldn't even think up the idea to do such a thing to another person." He told me one day a chaplain went through the compound asking the team to join in a praise and worship group later that night. A few hours later, my friend found himself sitting around a fire singing. He thought, *Why am I here? I don't know Jesus.* His status would soon change. "When faced with your own death daily in combat, it makes you see things. You see Jesus is what makes the difference," he explained to me.

The goal of evil is to instill fear, divide, lie, cheat, steal, and destroy. These brave peacemakers don't talk to their spouses and children about the horrors they see because they want to protect their loved ones. Evil lies and tells these brave peacemakers not to talk about what is destroying them or seek help, because if they do, they should think themselves weak. The evil can then steal who they are to destroy them through post-traumatic stress or isolation and divide their family. Maybe even cause them to take their own life.

My friend told me evil destroyed one of his teammates with post-traumatic stress disorder. His traumatized brother reached out to my friend because they had seen the same horror. He was wondering if my friend wasn't suffering from PTSD too.

"What did you say to him?" I asked.

He replied, "I told him I wasn't suffering the way he was, but I would be if it weren't for knowing Jesus. Jesus makes the difference."

When the rogue wave destroyed the *Anhinga*, we immediately lost all radio communications. Captain Eric's first response was to pick up the mic and call, "Mayday, mayday, mayday." We wanted help so badly, but we didn't have the ability to call for help. If you're suffering from a post-traumatic stress condition, if you think the world would be better off without you, or you are having some other suicidal thought that makes you feel like your ship is sinking, call for help before it's too late. It is okay to get help. Getting help is not weak, it's strong. Asking for help requires putting down the very pride that pushes you into a darker place. Transmit the personal mayday for a professional on this earth, and also to the One above.

That night around the campfire at the farm in Goochland with the members of the Virginia Beach Police made me realize something that stirred my soul. I listened to true stories where good officers testified they had witnessed evil beyond what's possible for a human being. To be clear, there is a lot of evil brought on by our own choices. But some soldiers experienced evil that was beyond our ability to create. If these brave men and women can testify that evil is real, *why can't they see God is real too?*

The sanctuary of Blackwater Baptist Church.

Jack (my son) and me at Fisherman's Wharf Marina, heading to the *Sniper* boat to see Captain Jimmy before going to an awards banquet. I was captain of the 60 Viking, *Episode*, and we had achieved second place in the BMO tournament for Mr. Haycox.

CHAPTER 21:

NO PROBLEM CRYING OUT

During the summer of 2012, I was faced with my ultimate fear: divorce.

I couldn't imagine anything worse in life than losing my family. This was not just an adult fear. It's something I had feared my entire life. The intensity of the grasp that this fear always had on my life was overwhelming. Was it born during an argument I had overheard between my parents when I was a little boy? My parents worked through any adversity with love and are still happily married.

The loss of my family meant I was a failure as a husband, father, and as a man. I never had an affair with another woman, but I had cheated on my wife with my job. Mostly, I failed to follow the direction God gave me. It was not on purpose. I failed to read His instruction manual for a wife.

Husbands, love your wives, as Christ loved the church and gave Himself up for her, that He might sanctify her, having cleansed her by the washing of water with the word, so that he might present the church to Himself in splendor, without spot or wrinkle or any such thing, that she might be holy and without blemish. In the same way husbands should love their wives as their own bodies. He who loves his wife loves himself. For no one ever hated his own flesh, but nourishes and cherishes it, just as Christ does the church, because we are members of His body. "Therefore a man shall leave his father and mother and hold fast to his wife, and the two shall become one flesh" (Ephesians 5:25-31 ESV).

I had been attacked at my most vulnerable area. I was at the lowest point I had ever sunk to in my life. Severely depressed, with no feeling of value in life at all, I had forgotten what the Lord had done for me on April 13, 1998. I felt like an even greater failure than I did when I was unable to find the EPIRB. I was taken back to the darkness. The thought of how much of my son's life I would have missed was devastating.

One day, while I was taking a shower, I fell to my knees and cried out to the Lord. I was lost and needed to know I was not alone, just as I needed to know I was not alone while shipwrecked ninety miles out in the Gulf Stream.

The storms and rough seas of life come at us in many different forms: divorce, cancer, the loss of a loved one, loss of a job, a child walking out of your life, or maybe addiction. When the *Anhinga* went down, it was like everything that was important to me was gone. The breath in my lungs was the only thing left, and that would soon cease to be as I died alone in the merciless tempest at sea.

Mercy is something that was paid for in blood. In the book of Mark chapter four, Jesus had been speaking to a large crowd beside the sea. Afterward, He asked His disciples to go to the other side of the sea. Some of those disciples were seasoned fishermen. The Bible recounts that while they were on the sea, a great gale arose, causing waves to break into the boat while Jesus was taking a nap.

The disciples cried out, "Teacher, do you care that we are perishing?"

Jesus awoke and told the roaring sea, "Peace! Be still!" And the sea became calm. To the disciples He said, "Why are you so afraid? Have you still no faith?"

I don't know what your storm is. Maybe your tempest is post-traumatic stress disorder (PTSD). I get it, and it took writing this book for me to come to terms with the impact all those hours of fighting and fear had on my mind. Every Christmas and April 13 since 1998, I have had to find somewhere to go and hide so I can try to cry out the emotions inside. Even last night I woke up from a nightmare where I was at the helm of a yacht with the owner and his friends on the bridge. Then a two-hundred-foot tall wave crested on top of us. I woke up right after saying, "There is nothing we can do, boys." When I remember who was with Eric and me, the fear and terror turn to calm and peace. I am blessed that my tears are of gratitude.

If your storm is PTSD, get professional help. More importantly, cry out to the one the disciples cried out to while they were in the boat during the storm. Jesus can say, "Peace! Be still!" to the storm in your life. He is the great restorer of broken people.

While on my knees in the shower with tears running down my face, through the Holy Spirit, I received a clear direction: "It's time to tell My story." Meaning His story. And as it is true with many of those who have been chosen by the Lord for a task, I said... *Nope!* Actually, I replied more like this: "Lord, I am not into glorifying myself." His response was, "You aren't glorifying you, you're glorifying Me." At the time of the divorce, little did I know the amazing plan of restoration that was to come.

Very rarely did I ever share the story of the *Anhinga*. It was one of those stories I tried to keep to myself because I wanted to be known for my fishing abilities, not because I went for a long swim. For years, I had been randomly told that I have a special calling on my life. "Okay, yeah right. Everyone has that, don't they!" I never understood until that night when I finally cried out. I understood that the probability of the fact that we were stumbled upon ninety miles offshore and rescued was near impossible. The part I was missing was how big the events were that happened while fighting for our survival in the rough seas. There were events that confirmed the reality of who God is.

He will never leave us regardless of how vast and empty the stormy seas are in front of us. There was also the powerful moment when He showed up as I was to take the only path I could see to bring an end to the overwhelming battle with the waves, ending myself. Through these events, I grew spiritually. It is a blessing to live every day being truly thankful for that day knowing I am not on this earth by my own will. I have the ability to live every day with zero fear of death because I was saved. Every day has been a gift from above since April 13, 1998.

After that encounter in the shower, I wondered if people were still talking about this event that changed the industry. It changed the sportfishing industry twenty years ago by alerting crews in the '90s that sometimes boats sank immediately with no time to gather stowed away safety gear. I did a Google search on the story of the *Anhinga* to find that the story was still being told but not in the same fashion. They talked about the boat and the surfboard, but there was no mention of the words that explained the miraculous rescue of the *Anhinga* crew after going down without a distress call. Those echoed words were, "God saved those boys out there."

Soon after this realization, I had a conversation with a friend who is an inshore guide in the Outer Banks of North Carolina and a broker with Mossy Oak Properties. It was put on his heart to start the Outer Banks Sportsmen's Fellowship. In a discussion we had about the calling that was placed on his life, Captain Bryan told me he didn't want to answer to Jesus one day why he didn't follow through with this calling. I was haunted, more like convicted, by the thought of what would happen if I didn't share the story about the miracles that occurred while lost at sea. God might find someone else. Like Bryan, I did not want to answer for that one day. God had literally saved me from the water and from death with His blood. It would be wrong not to follow through with His request to share the testimony.

The basis of the story was well-known by many, but the true heart penetrating details of the day were not. I had seen people spiritually moved during the few informal situations where the story was shared. The story had never been shared with a prayerful invitation for the Lord to use me as His vessel to speak to hearts. Then, out of the blue, I received a call from a fellow captain, Carson. He was in his Forrester Boatworks boat building shop and asked if I would come speak to a sportsmen's fellowship in Suffolk, Virginia. This would be the first formal speaking event and the first step toward fulfilling a promise I had made many years ago to share the testimony with my own home church.

After the call with Carson, I reflected on the recent informal times the story was told. In the past, many people had told me I should "write a book" about the struggle and survival that Captain Eric and I experienced. I realized in the recent time the story was shared, there was new meaning after I was able to see how it truly touched the lives of each person who heard it. Whether it's an ex-con or a naval special forces operator, it is truly God who touches the hearts, not me.

Through all of the pain and loneliness of divorce, I choose to take the difficult and narrow road. I was the captain of one of the nicest and fastest sportfishing yachts in Virginia. That alone could have easily allowed me the opportunity to take the wrong road. One of Virginia Beach's best wedding venues is located at Fisherman's Wharf Marina where the boat was docked. On any given weekend during the summer, the boat was next to a load of beautifully dressed intoxicated single women with love on their mind. Most of them had been leaning on the rail admiring the multimillion-dollar yachts. Some of my friends even encouraged me to go down the wide road that led away from the God who had rescued me.

One day, I received a call from Darren, my brother in-law, encouraging me to read the book of Job. After reading how he had lost everything and then was restored in abundance because of his faithfulness, I wanted that King of restoration in my life.

I was restored with an amazing wife and three daughters in addition to my son. The Hallmark movie makers would have a hard time creating a love story to match the one belonging to my wife and me. It started long before we could have ever imagined. When we were first starting to talk, I pulled out a box of old fishing pictures from my days of traveling in pursuit of marlin. There was a picture in the box of a twelve-foot johnboat on my neighbor's pond. It was my first boat, a gift from Grandaddy Jack. In the picture is a young boy paddling in the front of the boat while in the back is my neighbor holding a toddler girl. The little boy in the front of the boat is me. The little girl on her first boat ride is now my wife, Samantha. Her Aunt Sandy and Uncle Landy lived next door. I am a blessed man to have such a wonderful wife who supports and encourages the sharing of my testimony.

You have a testimony. If your testimony is not shared, it's not helping a brother or sister. *How many more people could have been helped if I would have started sharing the story of the* Anhinga *sooner? How many more lives would have been saved?*

CHAPTER 22:

TOUCHING OTHERS

"Count it all joy, my brothers, when you meet trials of various kinds, for you know that the testing of your faith produces steadfastness."

—JAMES 1:2-3 ESV

SUFFOLK, VIRGINIA

After I cried out and received the instruction to tell "my story," I failed to ask the big question: "How?" The "how" was soon answered through a phone call from a friend and fellow captain, Carson.

Carson is an Oregon Inlet captain who told me that his father was a member of an outdoors fellowship group that meets at a hunt club's building in Suffolk, Virginia. The group met monthly and needed a speaker in a couple months. Remembering the direction received through prayer, I agreed.

As a safety trainer, I knew a visual aid would be needed to enhance the experience for the audience. The presentation needed a means to convey the details of the sportfishing world to someone who has never been far out to sea or even on a sportfishing vessel. Mostly importantly, the audience would need to understand why I deemed our rescue a miraculous example of God's amazing love and grace, as I was certainly undeserving.

A couple of months passed by quickly, and the day I would formally share the story of the *Anhinga* arrived. I reviewed the details of the fight for survival as my son and I drove to the hunt club. To add to the challenge, they would be serving a meal at the beginning of the meeting. I would be speaking to a group of adults with full bellies. In other words, they were prepped for naptime.

Prior to stepping up to the microphone, I prayed that the Lord would make me His messenger. I wanted to touch hearts in the way they needed to be ministered to. As the story was being delivered, I had an urge to go off script. I told the true story in a way it had never been shared before. Everything I said was true, but I was emphasizing details in a deeper way. Heartfelt lessons learned from pain and suffering I had experienced over the past several months were included in the message.

It was working. The audience was focused. Their full bellies were forgotten. There were men with tears in their eyes, others had deep looks of contemplation. A sense of humbleness filled the room. I was absolutely exhausted as the message came to a conclusion two hours later.

I stepped away as the group's leader stepped up to the microphone to provide an invitation to the group, which included first-time guests and longtime members. With my head bowed, I thanked God for the opportunity and hoped I had effectively delivered His story.

I was amazed to see a line forming of people who wanted to speak to me. I was used to employees running out the door at the end of safety training classes, but these people were disinclined to leave. One by one, they shared the details of how my story had touched their hearts. In an instant, I knew I was not the one who had worked on their hearts. I was humbled and amazed. As soon as Jack and I closed the doors on the Ford F-350, I cried. My son saw the love of his father in the compassion I had for strangers in every tear that flowed off my cheeks.

I'm continually stunned by the effect of my testimony of being lost at sea. I never would've imagined that the love shown to me by the Father in ensuring we were rescued would aid so many in the rescue of their hidden emotions and sometimes of their souls. The following are just a few of the many stories of how the story of the *Anhinga* has touched others' lives.

MANTEO, NORTH CAROLINA:
Friend and first-class inshore fishing guide, Bryan, asked me to speak to a group of outdoorsmen. In the Outer Banks Sportsmen's Fellowship, there would be fellow captains and mates who I had the pleasure of working alongside out of the Oregon Inlet and Mexico. One of those in attendance was the same friend who rented a car and braved the dangerous stretch between Puerto Aventuras and Cancún to bring me a toothbrush.

The night prior to this outdoorsmen-speaking engagement, I called him to see if he could make it. Tears of gratitude came to my eyes when my friend said he could. His presence upped the emotional challenge of delivering the message. He told me he was unemployed from the boat he had been running for the past several years. The owner had sold it. He had been providing for his beautiful family by working as a freelance captain, performing boat maintenance and commercial fishing around Oregon Inlet. With a hint of hesitation in his voice, he told me about an opportunity that had come up to run a state-of-the-art brand-new sportfish boat for a private owner who paid well.

My friend went on to express his concerns about the new job requiring full-time travel mainly out of the country.

He took a deep pause and used that unique spin he jokingly puts on pronouncing my last name, saying, "Sav-auge, I'm afraid if I take this job, I might end up losing my family."

He knew my world was being ripped apart by divorce. We talked about how important it is to fight for your family. I understood the difficult situation he was in related to the risk of providing for his family. Similar to military families, it's difficult for traveling sportfishing crews to maintain their relationships.

While in route to Manteo the day I was to speak, the phone rang. It was Bryan.

"Johnny, there is something I have to tell you. The gentlemen in the front two rows will all be wearing Carolina-blue polo shirts. They are there by court order."

At the start of my speech, I prayed for God to use me as His messenger to touch hearts. The recovering drug addicts and alcoholics wearing Carolina-blue polos in the front two rows were taking handwritten notes like college students during a PowerPoint. I remember seeing this and thinking, *Dear Lord, what am I saying to touch them in such a way?*

When I finished, the leader stepped up to thank me and give an invitation to conclude. A line of sportsmen wanting to express their gratitude was forming in front of me. Through the crowd, I saw a gentleman get up from the rear of the hall and start making his way toward the podium. I had never seen him before in my life, but I knew his condition.

He was a commercial fisherman, my age from Wanchese, and he appeared to be clearly strung out on drugs. He walked right up to me and wrapped his arms around me. With a big hug, he said, "God sent you down here to talk to me."

After the line had dissipated, my friend who was contemplating what to do about his job approached and said, "Johnny, I decided I'm not taking the traveling job on the new boat. I love my family too much to risk losing them. I'm going to stay here and keep doing what I'm doing. The Lord will provide."

When I got in my truck, I cried again. This time I cried all the way back home.

PUNGO, VIRGINIA
A dear and close friend of mine, Billy, once asked me to share the story of the *Anhinga* with the middle and high school students in his youth group at Charity United Methodist Church in the rural Pungo area of Virginia Beach. When I stepped into the youth room, I could not help but notice a number of the boys were on the same baseball team as my son. The next thing I knew, the pastor had cancelled his adult Bible study, and they all joined the group. The pressure was on.

It was important for these teens to know they're loved. Our earthly fathers may fail, but our Heavenly Father will never fail us. When it feels like He's failing us, He isn't. He is allowing something to happen in our lives because He loves us and wants to bring us closer to Him. After finishing the story, the teens had some very good questions. Then Pastor Dave stood up and gave an invitation for the teens to accept Christ into their lives. Six of my son's teammates did. I cried all the way home.

HATTERAS, NORTH CAROLINA

The opportunities to share with young adults continued to include one of the most humbling and comical resulting testimonies I've ever had. The boss wanted to fish the Hatteras Marlin Club Blue Marlin Release Tournament. While on the Hatteras Marlin Club dock, I was approached by Earle. He is a friend and co-owner of Bluewater. He has always been a great advocate of sharing the miracle of the *Anhinga*. Earle wanted me to share the story with his children, Connor and Kelsea. I felt truly honored for the opportunity to do something for someone who had done so much for me over the years.

I asked him where he'd like to meet. He pointed to a sixty-four-foot Viking called the *Knot Done Yet*. My heart sank because I didn't know how I would be able to inspire hope in the presence of a man who defined never giving up. Mr. Nichols, the owner of the boat, was confined to an electric wheelchair due to muscular dystrophy. I had been watching him all week and noticed he was only physically confined to the chair. Mr. Nichols seemed to be so filled with joy as he watched the children playing in the bounce houses and the adults shuffling on the dance floor. I prayed, asking the Lord to use me to give hope to this man who had given me inspiration.

I struggled to maintain composure as the story was delivered. Thankfully, my friend Chip went along to provide moral support. I was incredibly humbled whenever I looked into Mr. Nichols's eyes. To refrain from breaking into tears, I shifted attention to the puppy being held by one of Kelsea's friends. The story came to a conclusion. I was thankful for the questions that followed about various parts of the experience. The questions helped me to know where gaps should be filled when sharing the testimony in the future.

The most thankful person for the story to end was probably Kelsea's friend who was holding the puppy. About halfway through the story, the puppy had peed in the young lady's lap, but she never moved. Her shorts and the towel in her lap were soaked in puppy pee. She could have asked for a timeout, but she didn't. It warmed my heart when she said she was too interested in the story to interrupt.

NORFOLK, VIRGINIA

There are many accounts of how the story has touched hearts and even more I'm unaware of. The next account is an example of how God has literally used the suffering Captain Eric and I endured to save a life. It took me a long time to learn to respond when He had placed something on the heart.

While lost at sea, I told myself that if I survived, I was going to go back to school. I returned to Old Dominion University to pursue a master's in public health, focused on safety and industrial hygiene. My education was put to use with Ford Motor Company at their Norfolk Assembly Plant until the plant closed and then for Virginia Paving Company as a safety manager.

I learned of an employee who had strained a muscle while lifting chunks of asphalt. The employee was a young, Black man who had seen his fair share of evil and hard times. The tattoos covering both of his arms told a story of street smarts, toughness, and pain. Knowing this man in his mid-twenties had served time in jail, I was somewhat nervous for my own safety.

As can be expected, he ended up in my office as part of the investigation process to determine the cause and how to prevent similar incidents in the future. My wonderful wife had decorated my office in an array of offshore fishing pictures from over our years. One morning, while fishing in the Virginia Beach Invitational Marlin Tournament, she actually had me change course so she could get the perfect picture of the sunrise through the portside outrigger. I'm glad I listened to her because the large print of the photo became the focus of the injured employee's attention. I paused the investigation.

The Spirit within me was prompting me, "Share my story."

I listened and began to share the story of the *Anhinga*. This time, it weighed heavy on my heart to share what it was like out there, lonely and being struck by the whitecaps of huge, breaking waves. Never before had I been pressed to share what it was like to be tossed around underwater, held down, and then coming up gasping for a gulp of air in my lungs.

I noticed tears forming in the eyes of this hardened young man who was sitting on the other side of my desk. I thought, *Dear lord, how are you using me to touch his heart?* I struggled to hold my own tears of compassion as I continued the details of how Captain Eric and I relentlessly fought for our survival.

Then, he broke. The ex-convict had a river of tears flowing from his eyes. He gasped as he balled in front of me. I was at a total loss for what I should do. Should I keep on with the story or ask how he could be helped? The best thing I could think to do at the moment was to give him the clean paper towel on my desk. He accepted.

He looked straight into my eyes with tears still flowing and said, "Mr. John, I tried to kill myself yesterday. I took a whole bottle of pills, but it didn't work." Immediately, I jumped up and ran around my desk to embrace him. His body went limp in my arms as I assured him that he is loved.

I then asked him to sit back down so I could go to the other end of our office building to inform my boss we had an employee who needed immediate help.

Lonnie dropped everything he was doing and ran to my office. He, too, embraced the young man. The employee was enrolled into an assistance program. His physical pain from the muscle strain was a mere scratch compared to the hidden emotional pain he held within.

The young man and I stopped at a bookstore when taking him home after work that day. We went inside, and he picked out a Bible. The young man had told me about how much he enjoyed his mother taking him to church when he was younger.

Several months later, he went on to work for another employer with a schedule more suited for him to help take care of his brother and sister. I guess it was about a year later when I received a call from the receptionist saying there was a visitor in the lobby. The man who appeared before me was a completely different one from the man who'd once broken down across from me at my desk. The young man had a glow of joy this time.

He gave me a big hug and said, "I came here to thank you for what you did for me. My life has changed, and I am doing well."

I smiled and simply replied with the truth. "Thank you, but it wasn't me or Lonnie. I was just the messenger. It was the one who inspired the book we bought taking you home that day who deserves the credit."

When the tough young man broke down in my office that day, he was crying out for help. If you're struggling today, don't let pride keep you from reaching out. You were uniquely created to be loved. Know you are loved even though it may seem impossible because you feel you're unworthy. Remember, there is a single book that has many of the answers to the trials and temptations of life. It's the one we picked for the distressed young man.

BOAT CHURCH, VIRGINIA BEACH

Captain Eric and I are truly only the messengers for the story of the *Anhinga*. We were saved to give others hope. I was just a messenger sharing a miraculous story from a boat on the water when a hopeless hospital administrator was touched. He drove from the mountains to Virginia Beach for the weekend to escape the tribulations of staffing and managing a hospital during COVID-19. He sat on the beach listening to a story about two men who endured a trial to keep their heads above water and air in their lungs. After breaking into tears and reflecting on the moral of never giving up, he returned to the mountains with a new inspiration.

The story of the *Anhinga* has touched many people, from the hearts of police officers around a campfire, to US Navy SEALs from kitchen tables, to a daughter's softball team party. The events I have just shared are just a few of the stories about how the testimony of the *Anhinga* has touched and changed lives. Collectively, the questions and feedback from those touched have been an inspiration that helped me to overcome my biggest fear related to writing this book. I was afraid I might not include a unique detail that was needed to provide hope to aid just one reader.

There was a perfect plan at work for Captain Eric and me to be rescued from the grips of the sea. A plan was also in play for the story of the *Anhinga* to touch hearts through this book. Many audience members had suggested writing a book, but I didn't know how it would be possible. This answer would come when my wife made arrangements to meet one of her old friends at a Mexican restaurant. Her friend, Tiffany Mosher, is the author of *Beauty Beyond the Threshold*. Tiffany put me on the course to meet the request I had heard so often. I knew to write this book, I would have to recall the details by revisiting the very fight for survival and the thing I feared the most. It was not being lost at sea.

Captain Johnny Savage as a boy who did not want to quit fishing to go home. Not much has changed.

CHAPTER 23

IN THE ADMIRAL'S HANDS

"For what does it profit a man to gain the whole world and forfeit his soul?"
—MARK 8:36 ESV

The devil and his cohort of fallen angels wait for opportunities to use our thoughts of darkness and despair to further destroy us. This is exactly what was happening to me while out at sea. When I had paddled out the second time looking for the EPRIB, my thoughts evolved from those of hope in "Our Father who art in heaven" to thoughts of whether God was even real in my weakened state. I began to question why He could not or would not save us.

The part of the story when I decided to commit suicide was very difficult to share. My wife said I woke up screaming three times the night after it was written. I once heard Pastor Chuck Swindoll say something to the effect of how he was convinced suicide is demonic. I believe him. The way my thought patterns led me to rationalize the ending of my life was not who I am. One of my best friends committing suicide confirmed for me that we are easy prey when we are hopeless.

Even in the darkest of nights, there is always hope. The amazing thing about light is that even a speck of it can push away the dark. If you have ever or are considering suicide, do not do it. The effects suicide has on your surviving family and friends are awful. You're valued even if it may not seem like it in the moments of distress. There is a way out. Tell someone you trust, and seek professional help. Most importantly, seek the One who loves you more than any other. Do not cut God short on His plan for your life as I almost did. My family has sacrificed much over the past year for this book to be written. All of the nightmares from revisiting April 13, 1998, and the missed family functions are all worth it if the story of the *Anhinga* helps to save even one more life.

As I mentioned earlier in the book, for many years it was rare for me to tell the story of the *Anhinga*. It was even more rare that I had the courage to share what happened when I tried to commit suicide. The voice I heard was there and was true. I don't fully understand everything about what happened when I heard the voice while alone in the middle of a storm. Was it the angel of the Lord that showed up, stopping my death? I don't know. I'm just thankful they did.

The most repeated command in the Bible is "fear not." When angels visually appear to people in the Bible, they often start the conversation with "Fear not." God wants us to trust Him and not be afraid. Possibly, the voice I heard when I was about to commit suicide was the archangel like Michael or maybe Gabriel, whom God uses as messengers in the Bible, or some other angel. Maybe it was Jesus. I am not sure who or what the voice came from, but I am certain they were there with me. Why did I only hear the voice and not see its source? Possibly, I didn't see it because the fear I already had of getting eaten by sharks had overwhelmed me to the point of taking my own life. I think if an angel would have visually appeared, it would have been more than my fear gauge could have handled at the time. There's no question that I heard the sound in my ear and the voice came from behind my right shoulder.

I knew the level of my directional capabilities; therefore, it was not possible for me to establish a sense of which way to go on my own. This is in reference to following the instruction of "pick your line and paddle it." The underlying ground swell combined with the wind-generated waves created a wave pattern where their angles crossed. It made for an extremely confusing sea surface condition. With help from above, I found a pattern in the confused sea condition to allow me to paddle directly back to Captain Eric over such a long distance. Being able to set a course and paddle directly back to Captain Eric without having any source of reference to establish direction was truly a miracle in itself.

I never understood the true significance of the words spoken to me until about two years ago. It hit me like someone turning on the light switch in a dark room. My slight fear of someone questioning what I know as the truth of hearing a voice saying, "John, you have spent a lot of time out here. Pick your line and paddle it." The verification of the truth is in the Bible. Trust me, I would not have known this in 1998, because I never read my Bible.

What I heard can be broken into three parts. The first is comfort. "John, you have spent a lot of time out here." I was scared enough to kill myself. When one unexpectedly calls our name, we're automatically comforted with familiarity.

It's personal, and it stops us in our tracks. They know us. I was scared and needed comfort.

There are many stories in the Bible where the angel shows up and provides a message with two clear statements. The Divine Intervention was reassured upon realizing that I had also received the two consistent statements from the messenger who stopped my suicide. It was so clear that it was like the light switch had been turned on. One of the examples is in Genesis 19, where Lot is instructed to take his wife and two daughters away from Sodom. They are instructed to flee from Sodom and Gomorrah and to not look back. There was a *direction or heading* to go and an *instruction*.

"Pick your line" was my direction or heading. There was a path made visible in the confused action of the waves that was beyond my ability to recognize. "...And paddle it" was my instruction. I was no longer lost out there in the Gulf Stream and now in the sea of life. This allowed me to see the truth in how God speaks to us through His word, the Bible.

You may or may not believe the part of the story where God, Jesus, the Holy Spirit, or an angel showed up and stopped my attempted suicide. Your belief in that part of the story may rest in whether or not you think I'm an honest person. I'm okay with that because I know I was in my right mind at the time. I know my body filled with warmth and strength from the tips of my fingers to the tips of my toes with all motor skills fully functional. I know what I heard, the direction it came from, and the wonderful voice that was in my ear.

One of Satan's favorite tactics for pulling us away from God is to make us question if God actually exists. I tell you that God is as real as I am sitting here right now in a camper typing these words. Why He chose to save me out there, I will never understand until I fall on my knees at the feet of Jesus face to face. I certainly wouldn't have chosen to save me out of the life I was living. I was living a selfish life of fishing hard all day and partying all night.

Captain Eric and I know there is absolute truth in the existence of a mighty and loving Creator. When the *Anhinga* was struck by the rogue wave on April 13, 1998, at about 8:50 a.m., we were approximately ninety nautical miles west-southwest of Key West, Florida. The wind was blowing from the east-southeast toward the west-northwest while we were submersed in the Gulf Stream current. The current flows in an east-northeasterly direction, according to general knowledge, and is identified as such on National Oceanic and Atmospheric Administration (NOAA) Nautical Charts. The Gulf Stream flows like a river through the ocean.

According to the science, Captain Eric and I should have drifted to the northeast with the Gulf Stream, which would have carried us up between the East Coast of Florida and the western side of the Bahama Islands. This was the area where we had the greatest chance of being eaten alive by the sharks.

Wind drift is another factor to consider about our illogical location. Objects like our coolers and poly-balls that are on the surface of the ocean can be pushed by the wind. The less drag they have in the water, the faster they will be taken in a downwind direction. Our bodies were submerged in the water; therefore, the effects of being blown across the surface of the water would have been hardly detectable. It is possible for the wind to blow hard enough to push the actual surface water in a downwind direction. In this case, Captain Eric and I would have drifted up into the Gulf of Mexico in a northwesterly direction, adding current would have likely put us on northern drift.

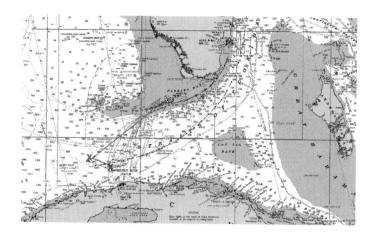

The fact is, to the best of our knowledge, Eric and I drifted approximately twenty miles to the southeast. We were drifting into the wind and across the Gulf Stream, which was flowing to the east-northeast. The captain and I were placed directly in the path of the only other boats on April 13, 1998, making the 350-mile journey from Key West, Florida, to Cancún, Mexico. We were placed dead center on the heading of a boat that chose to alter course because of bad weather. If the vessel the *Ditch Digger* or *Sans Souci* would have been delayed by five minutes, they would have received the message from Hacienda Del Mar, "It's getting bad over here. Don't send any boats."

Scientifically and meteorologically, it should have been near impossible that we were found. I'm not a statistical probabilities expert, but as a captain, I can tell you the chances of us being found before dark out there in such a great expanse with no known last point of contact was pretty much impossible.

Captain Eric and I are here today because God chose to work a miracle in our lives. His reason for saving us is beyond my ability to understand, but I don't think the purpose is for me to fully understand. Maybe the purpose of our rescue was for me to help you see how the admiral's love is working in your life.

Photo taken in 2015 when Samantha and I were returning home from our honeymoon. We stopped in Stuart, Florida, to visit Captain Eric.

CHAPTER 24:

CROSSING THROUGH DANGEROUS WATERS

> *"For God so loved the world, that he gave his only Son, that whoever believes in him should not perish but have eternal life."*
> —JOHN 3:16 ESV

The Bible is full of true stories about how people have asked, then trusted God and waited for amazing things to happen in His time. I had to be broken to see and put away my selfishness; then I cried out for help. That is how I was able to see His power in the testimony of the *Anhinga*. He has refined but not changed the story over the past few years since April 13, 1998.

Satan knows the days are numbered for himself and his cohort of fallen angels, so his goal is to try to hurt God by trying to the destroy what God loves most of all—us. The devil also knows there is power in our testimony. Delivering my testimony certainly has not been very easy. It seems like evil has come against me in different ways, attempting to stop the sharing of the testimony you have just read. If Satan can stop the message from spreading about the truly wonderful things God has done in our lives, evil has won. Do not be afraid to share your testimony. There's nothing on this earth more valuable than a soul.

We live in a fallen world. Sometimes these bad things are the result of choices we make, sometimes they're the evil in this world that's clawing at us, and sometimes it's part of God's plan to sanctify us. In the end, the devil loses and will pay for all the pain and suffering brought to this world. I don't know the struggles you may have had, are having, or will have. Struggles are a certainty in this life. The course you take through your struggles will determine how you come out in the end. You are not alone in the dark times when you feel like you have no hope. He is with you the same way He was with Captain Eric and me the whole time we were fighting for our lives.

In the world of being a safety engineer, I often wonder how many more times people will break their backs because they refuse to ask for help carrying the load. Why do so many people resist asking for help when they already know they can't handle the load? Pride has been the demise of many since the beginning of time.

A few chapters ago, I mentioned the dangers of running through the Oregon Inlet and Hatteras Inlet of the North Carolina's Outer Banks. The fleets that fish out those inlets have captains who are more than willing to share their local knowledge of the inlet's condition. They share exactly which buoys to stay away from, which to hug, and even the spot where the channel is outside of the buoy line. In addition, the US Army Corps of Engineers conducts hydrographic surveys to determine the location of the channel or deepest water for boats and yachts to safely travel through. With a little planning and a quick phone call, a captain can safely navigate through the most hazardous waters on the East Coast.

Some captains don't take the time to plan for their voyage through the dangerous waters. There are also captains who are too proud to pick up the phone and ask for the information gained by the sacrifices of another. As a result of refusing to ask for this gift, the vessel is in danger of running aground, which may cause injury or death to everyone on board the vessel.

Our life is like the open ocean with many choices of paths to take. At some point in time, we must cross through the dangerous waters. The shoals and sandbars of life, including the biggest problem with life, has already been put on the charts. The biggest problem in life is death, which is a navigational hazard we will all meet one day. The question is, will you let pride stand in your way of safely going home to glory? Or will you accept the gift of the sacrifice already made that will get you to the glorious home?

Jesus already went through the worst of all shoals for all of us. He then drew a simple chart in His blood to show all how to safely deal with the worst of navigation hazards: death.

I don't know if you have accepted Him into your heart and life. Don't be like the captain who didn't plan before crossing the shoals and sandbars. Once you have run aground, it's too late. The wise captain asks for help!

If pride is holding you back from believing Jesus is real, think about the story you have just read. I promise you that He is real, and He loves you even when you do not understand.

As someone once told a friend and fellow captain who was dying of stage four cancer, "Accept the gift. You're dying. What do you have to lose?"

God knows your heart. If you would like to be certain that you will safely cross over and would like to accept Jesus as your savior, please, ask God to save you, and His Spirit will come into your life.

Heavenly Father,
I know that I am a sinner and I ask for your forgiveness. I believe Jesus died for my sins and rose from the dead. I am sorry for my sins and repent. I invite you to come into my heart and life. I want to follow Jesus as my Savior from this moment forward. Thank you for hearing my prayer.
In Jesus's name,
Amen.

By trusting Christ to save you, the angels in heaven are rejoicing. Find a Bible-believing church and fellowship. Also, please share your testimony of how you came to know Jesus.

If you have never trusted Christ, always know you are valuable and loved. Please open your eyes to see. I'm praying and asking others to pray the Lord will make Himself known to you.

If you have already accepted Jesus, brothers and sisters, please pray for each other, for those who have just accepted Jesus Christ and for those who hopefully will before they must cross the great sandbar. I would also appreciate prayers for my family and me.

Time is one of the most precious things on earth. I want to thank everyone for investing their time in reading a true story written by a simple fisherman.

Not the end, but the beginning of a new life.

"*Follow me, and I will make you fishers of men.*"
– MATTHEW 4:19 ESV

After my first marriage ended, I was determined to be as faithful to the Lord as I could possibly be. I was blessed to receive a wife and new family. (Left to right: Jack, Meadow, Me, Samantha, Genevieve, and Brooklyn.)

PART 4:

APPENDIX OF STORIES— ADVENTURES OF THE GOON

There have been several places throughout the book where it is mentioned I did not deserve to be saved. As a mate, I worked hard and played hard. The two stories in this appendix are from a time when I was not exactly walking the path of my Christian roots.

My kids have always liked the funny short films at the end of some children's movies. When my son was a toddler, he was all about Walt Disney's *Cars* movie. We must have watched it five hundred times. We couldn't wait to see the Screamin' Banshee one more time.

We've had to cover some pretty serious stuff in this book. My wonderful wife and I wanted to leave you with a reason to laugh before finishing. So here are a couple stories about the adventures of the Goon, which is the name given to what I turn into when I've had a little too much to drink. When my wife, Samantha, and I started dating, she heard some of the myths about the wild and crazy antics of the Goon of my younger days. After hearing the stories, she really wanted to see the Goon. Well, one night at my friend Jason's wedding, she was able to meet the Goon. The next morning, she looked at me and said, "Don't you even let that thing back out again."

The Goon has been kept away since that day and it will stay away because it's important for me to maintain control of myself in order to maintain my witness. However, I hope you enjoy these fish stories about a fisherman who was in the process of finding his way.

FISH STORY 1:

MONKEY BUSINESS

Puerto Aventuras (PA) life in the '90s was truly an adventure. There was rarely a dull moment for owners, guests, and crews who visited the private resort located about fifty miles south of Cancún. The beaches and reef were beautiful, the restaurants were great, and there were always plenty of activities. There were bonds like brothers created between the fisherman who called the paradise home for a couple months each spring.

The resort had so much action going on, except the nightlife was limited to the Discoteca. It was a happening club filled with a bunch of buzzed fishermen, but the dude to chick ratio was about ten to one. Puerto Aventuras was like an island surrounded by Yucatan jungle, and like an island, if you don't bring it you aren't going to get it.

About nine miles up the road was a Mexican tourist town called Playa Del Carmen. This town is in the heart of Riviera Maya. It's just a taxicab ride away to hotels, beaches, bars, and babes. We would generally start off north and work our way to the south, barhopping our way down to Carlos and Charlie's. We called it Chuck and Chuck's, but today it's Senor Frog's.

It probably wasn't smart to down a couple caipirinhas before the Playa Del Carmen adventure. A caipirinha, Brazil's national cocktail, was served in what appeared to be a small fishbowl. The liquor in Brazil's national cocktail is cachaca, which is added to ice, limes, and sugar. That's right, no mixer. It wasn't pretty by the time we reached the final stop in Playa.

As we approached Chuck's in the spring of 1997, there it was, the object of our shenanigans for the night, just sitting there on a cinderblock wall. Freddie noticed it too. I could tell he was thinking the same thing. *We have to get this back to the marina. We'll be legends of Puerto Aventuras for generations to come if we can steal that monkey sitting over there and get it back to the compound.* After all, one of the theme songs for PA that year was Peter Gabriel's "Shock the Monkey."

We may or may not have been a little drunk when this idea popped into our heads. As the rest of our small group continued ahead into Chuck's, Freddie and I hooked left toward the two-block tall wall. We sat down on each side of the monkey as if we had approached an old friend. I thought, *Now what are we going to do?*

Freddie made the first move. He was on the other side taking his shirt off. It was a brilliant idea. We would disguise the monkey. As soon as Freddie finished putting his shirt on the monkey, I took my hat off and put it on its head. No one would ever know it was a monkey now. To solidify this assurance, Freddie and I started to carry on a conversation with the monkey.

All of a sudden, our plan appeared to be in danger as two Federales with M-16 machine guns started walking our way. The only thing more dreaded than ending up in a Mexican hospital was a Mexican jail. It became painfully evident they were onto us as they came closer. When the M-16 toting police were about forty feet away, Freddie and I made a break for it.

Freddie broke left and I grabbed the monkey, put it under my left arm, and made a break to the right. The Federales were in hot pursuit yelling for us to stop. I knew there were too many people around for them to start shooting. Then came the exfiltration plan to get myself out of the hostile area. I knew there were taxi cabs lined up only two city blocks over to the northwest of my position.

I was able to put some distance between myself and machine guns. As I reached the taxi cab staging area, a driver was opening the back door for the first person in the line of tourists waiting to be taken back to their hotel. I cut the line and dove into the back seat with the monkey still under my left arm. When the driver saw the US hundred-dollar bill fly into the front seat, he slammed the door shut and ran around to dash us out of there.

We made it back to PA, and the monkey ended up on somebody's boat tied up on the top landing of their tuna tower. When I woke up the next morning, I had no clue where the monkey or Freddie had ended up, but I somehow knew it had been a good night.

As I confessed the previous night's insurrection to my Mexican friend, Pancho, he started laughing. There was absolutely nothing funny about being a fugitive of justice.

"This isn't funny. I'll never be able to go to Playa again. They'll arrest me. The Federales had to have recognized me as a pescador. They might even look here. Stop laughing!" I said.

Pancho replied, "Garfish, they just wanted your money. The Federales can't do anything to you for stealing a monkey. You could have only been arrested if you had drugs."

"Really? That's cool!"

The pet sunglasses-stealing monkey at Papaya Republic ("The Monkey Bar") down the beach at Puerto Aventuras. This is not the stolen monkey that went for a ride in the taxi cab.

FISH STORY 2:

THE PRINCESS, THE GOLDFISH, AND THE BLEEDING MACKEREL

Thanks to the grace of God, I was able to end up working on the brand-new Viking for Captain Steve. This story took place about six hundred miles east-southeast of Virginia Beach. It may still be legend on the island of Bermuda.

The island of Bermuda is absolutely beautiful, and the blue marlin fishing was great. The run to the marlin fishing ground was short, but the fuel was expensive. The fuel cost for a day of fishing was about equal to the cost of fishing out of the mid-Atlantic with our longer run to the continental shelf. As an incentive to get American boats to fish in Bermuda, fuel was duty-free when filling up the tanks to run back across the Atlantic.

The charter fishing fleet is relatively small, which made the fishermen there very close knit. King of the charter fleet is legendary Captain Allen Desilva, with his record blue marlin of 1,325 pounds. There is another Allen Desilva who also blue marlin fished on the banks of Bermuda. One was known as "Good Allen" and the other "Bad Alan." The good one must have been the one with the big fish. But both are really great men.

Bermuda is a British territory where everyone I met was very nice. The people of Bermuda are proud of their island and take pride in keeping it clean. Keeping it clean is more than just disposing of trash. At the time, it was against the law to walk down the street in Bermuda without a shirt on, or so I was told. Prior to heading over, I had to go buy a new dress set of clothes, including a sport coat just to go to dinner.

Back in 1999, there were not very many marinas with full-service docks in Bermuda to tie up the *Chaos*. We were able to get dockage at the Hamilton Princess Hotel, where we had to tie up to a concrete wall on the broad Hamilton Harbour. We had to place large rubber inflated balls along the side of the boat toward the wall to keep the boat from getting beat up by wakes.

The *Chaos* was owned by two partners. Bill and "Rockin' Rod" were both so much fun to work for. Over the couple of years that I was their mate, it was a wonderful thing to see their love for fishing. When it came to going out and having fun, Bill was a professional. He had never been sauced when we went out to party. "Rockin' Rod" didn't drink when we would go out, but he sure would encourage his crew to when we didn't have to fish the next day. He encouraged it so much that he came up with a name for who or what I turned into. He called it the "Goon." Once he would get me intoxicated to the point that I turned into the Goon, he would reach into his pocket and give the Goon something that was like a quarter stick of dynamite and a lighter. I don't know what he saw so funny in this, but he sure would laugh. I'm surprised I still have all my fingers.

We caught a lot of fish and had a lot of laughs, like when Bill's friend, Frank, wore a stinky necklace made of squid skirts and chunks of garlic all day. He was having some bad blue marlin luck and that was the fix. Not really, but it sure was funny. His luck did change, though. Years after the stinky necklace, Frank and I became good friends.

The July moon blue marlin bite was over, and we had been in Bermuda for a few weeks. When the blue marlin fishing was hot, we had great luck on a fourteen-inch-long lure that was red, orange, and black. "Rockin' Rod" called it the "Bleeding Mackerel." It was about time for us to run back across the Atlantic to the United States. We had to be back in time to unload our deck fuel tank, resupply the boat, and run down to Manteo, North Carolina, for the Pirates Cove Big Game, Blue Marlin Tournament. Three days before we were departing, a strong wind came in, so we all had to cancel our trips for the next day. When the wind was blowing a gale and we didn't have to fish the next day, it was party time.

After dinner, we went to the Pickled Onion where the crew of the *Chaos* laid claim to the far side of the bar. I informed Suzanne that tonight was the night I was going to get her man back for assisting "Rockin' Rod" in making the Goon come out. She laughed. Rightly so, because I had tried just about every known mixture to get him drunk, but it never worked. I knew they had been out exploring the island that day, so he started a little early.

Then it was my turn for the round. I told the bartender two boilermakers each. I thought, *What did I just do? A tall glass of beer with a shot glass of whiskey dropped in it? That's gross, and I've never had one before in my life.* The look in Bill's eyes when he turned around and saw two and two glasses sitting on the bar was worth it. He was in terror but too proud to say "no."

We downed the boilermakers. It worked. Bill was utterly intoxicated, and I got myself crushed in the process. We ended up separating until about 3:00 a.m. when we all reconvened back at the boat. The rest of the *Chaos* fishing team was already on the boat hanging out in the cockpit when I returned.

Bill asked, "Goon, where have you been?" as I walked up to the stern wearing nothing but a bath towel from the hotel's pool.

"I went swimming, boss." The only problem was I was bone dry. To this day I don't know where I had been or where my clothes went. I do know there has never been another boilermaker.

In Bill's effort to get me back, he asked, "Hey, Goon. Did you see the pond filled with the fourteen-inch koi fish up by the hotel? I bet one would look good rigged for a blue marlin bait."

The Goon's eye lit up as Captain Steve's girlfriend, Deirdre, handed over an eight-foot gaff. The Hamilton Princess was one of the nicest resorts on the island. There was a courtyard in the center that had a tropical jungle with a babbling brook running through it. A little wooden foot bridge crossed over the stream that was fed by the koi pond at the head.

The Goon grabbed the gaff and took off down the tropical path, over the bridge, and to the Koi Pond. Still only wearing a towel on an island where it's illegal to walk down the street without a shirt. The Goon was mesmerized by all the potential baits swimming around him as he waded through the pond. While looking for the perfect live replica of the "Bleeding Mackerel," he failed to recognized the plate glass window ten feet away that lined the far side of the pond. On the other side of the glass was the restaurant and main lobby of the resort. Everyone on the other side of the translucent barrier was watching a mostly naked man standing in the middle of the shallow hotel koi pond.

There it was, the perfect bait. The Goon's eyes had a missile lock on his prize as he waded over with the stealth of a great blue heron and the determination for attack of a jaguar. Next the gaff was slowly lifted with the three-inch hook extended above and past the "Bleeding Mackerel's" living twin. Then, with a swipe like a flash of lightning, the point of the gaff stuck it just behind the pectoral fin. The Goon had it. There was no time to delay getting flopping fricassee to the bait cooler on the *Chaos*.

The Goon had the koi in his left hand and the gaff in his right as he made a dash down the path back to the boat through the tropical jungle. He rounded the corner and started over the babbling brook bridge. At full throttle, the Goon and an enormous security guard smashed into each other on the top of the bridge. They both screamed like girls because they'd scared each other so badly.

The security guard asked, "What are you doing with that fish?"

Without a pause, the Goon replied, "My boss wanted to see it. It's still alive. See this 'U' shape on the end of the pole? I used it to scoop up the fish. He's fine," I said as blood dribbled off the Goon's hand.

"Put it back," the giant said.

"Yes, sir." The Goon had finally been caught red handed. Literally.

The fish was released back into the pond. The defeated Goon returned to the *Chaos* with only the gaff and the towel he was wearing. The Goon arrived back at the boat and placed the gaff in the rod holder. He mumbled a few words, went inside, and climbed into his bunk.

"Rockin' Rod" had departed the action early the night before, so he was up early the next morning. Rod and Bill both roomed in the Princess. "Rockin' Rod"'s first stop the next morning was the front desk. The one in the lobby right next to the koi pond.

"Do I have any messages?" Rod asked.

"Yes, you do," responded the lady behind the desk. "One of your crew was very naughty last night."

When I woke up, the first thing I thought was, *Where did this towel come from, and why does my hand stink like fish? Oh no. That's right, the Goon came out last night.* Captain Steve was already up in the galley when I heard the distinctive slide of a Viking salon door. It was "Rockin' Rod".

All I could think was, *I'm going to get fired.*

In a deep, unamused voice, Rod said, "What in the world did y'all do last night?"

I could tell the captain was trying to maintain his composure when he replied, "The Goon got drunk and stuck a koi in the pond to put out as a bait on the short-rigger."

There was a moment of silence. Then they busted out laughing.

The wind was still blowing. The entire fleet was ashore, so they decided to all get together for a send-off lunch. Although embarrassed at my actions, I was still feeling a little defeated from the failure to complete my koi mission as I walked up the stairs to the second floor where the local fleet was waiting at the bar. As I rounded the top of the stairs, there sat the legendary Captain Allen Desilva.

"What did you do last night, Goon?" the captain shrieked out with his unique accent.

"How did you find out? It just happened this morning," I replied. At the bar, the whole fleet laughed. I couldn't help but start laughing too.

"The entire island of Bermuda knows about it," he replied with a big smile. "Johnny, those things are insured for $350,000.00."

Suddenly, I did not think it was funny anymore.

And that is the legend of the Princess, the Goldfish, and the Bleeding Mackerel.

Captain Steve (rear) and I (front) "creeking" Suzanne (flying) in the pool at Bermuda's Hamilton Princess Hotel. A "creeking" is a ceremony performed after someone catches their first marlin where they are thrown off the dock and into the water. Suzanne is the boss's wife, so we were nice and threw her in the pool.

ACKNOWLEDGMENTS

Heavenly Father, thank You for stirring my soul to share Your story that night on the *Desperado*. You know my spelling is terrible, and I do not write creatively very well, but You call on the least of us. Forgive me for telling You "no" a few years ago when You first told me to share Your story. When this writing process first started, I prayed, "God, I need Your help with this. Please put the right people in the right places." You answered that prayer, and in the process, You proved Your reality is as strong as that day in the sea. Thank You for giving Alan Jackson, Carrie Underwood, and Jason Gray the talent and desire to sign Your music. It brought additional peace when writing this story.

Now, I pray that You will place a hedge of protection around this book, me, my wife, the rest of my family, and all who use this book as a means to share Your gospel. I ask this in Jesus's name.

Samantha, your beauty is internal as much as it is external. Thank you for all of the sacrifices you have made during the writing process. Thank you for always encouraging me to write when I didn't want to. I do not understand how every time I speak, you are there listening as if you have never heard the story before. Thank you for putting up with all the sleepless nights. I love you with everything I am.

Jack, Brooklyn, Meadow, and GG, thank you for the sacrifices each of you made while I was writing this book. Let's go have some fun. You're all part of the reason for writing this book. I wanted y'all to always have the story of how good God is so you know where to look during your storms of life.

Mom and Dad, thank you for always being loving parents. I know it wasn't very easy, especially when you had no idea what country I was even in sometimes. Thank you for making me go to church even when I didn't want to.

To the rest of my extended family, I love you, and thank you for always being there.

Blackwater Baptist Church family, thank you for the love y'all continuously share.

Captain Eric Bingham, we will always have a connection that can never be broken. Thank you for mentally going back to that day in the water to help recall some of the details.

To the ex-Marine, ex-TEAM 2 guy, and the police officers who opened up the closet where the darkness is to help me to understand, thank you for your sacrifice.

Thank you to everyone who helped provide the details to complete this project. Beta readers, you were awesome. Thank you!

To the Creators Institute and New Degree Press Team, thank you so much for the opportunity to share this story of hope with the world. Eric, you have birthed an amazing process to provide others with a sense of accomplishment. Sherman and Bianca, both of you are simply amazing. There is absolutely no way this project could have been completed without your recommendations. This book was certainly a team effort.

I would like to thank the Virginia Paving Co. team—Lonnie, Julia, Josh, and Michelle—for carrying the additional load while this was being written.

Dave, thank you and Virginia Beach Law Group so much for the continuous encouragement and advice.

To all the supporters who financially and prayerfully contributed to the process, I was truly humbled to tears by your generosity. Thank you for believing in the power of the story of the *Anhinga*. If even one life is saved by this book, it is greater than all the riches on this earth.

Top Dog, you, Sir, are a great man. Thank you!

Captain VJ Bell, thank you for coming through with the Jim Smith Tournament Boats picture needed for the cover.

Ricky, Earle, Rudy, and Barry, learning of what each of you were doing behind the scenes to ensure this book was possible at the highest level made every struggle to catch a breath of air while battling the waves worth it. Thank you!

BOOK CONTRIBUTORS

Alice & Austin Savage
Alicia & Rick James
Andrea Medina
Angela Gregory
Angela Ward
Ashley Keech Beane
Ashley & Jeffrey Smith
Ashley & John Robert Wood
Barbara Feller
Billie Roney
Billy Conboy
Blake Harrison
Bobby Krivohlavek
Bonnie & Craig Talley
Brandon Ryan Horsley
Breanna & Marshall Hill
Brittaney & Jimmy Kovacs
Candace Seymore
Caroline & Jay Buffington
Carrie & Mike "Bubblegum" Merritt
Carrie & Jay Sawyer
Cindy & Frank Willson
Chad Ballard
Christopher Ryan
Crystal Gwaltney

Dale Pope
Danielle & Sean Jennings
David Harris
David Theiman
Dena & Sean Sawyer
Donald Arth
Doug Wilson
Denise & Earle Hall
E. G. Middleton III
Eric Koester
Erin Evans
Frederick 'Skipper" Feller
Garnet & Gary Gilmore
George Pilkington
Grant Lupien
Heather & Kevin Newton
Heather Schneider
Holy Campbell
Ingrid Holmes
Jake Keech
Jane & Howard Hill
Jeff Crooks
Jennifer Creech
Jennifer Wallace
Jessica & Chris Henry
Joe & Beverlee Woodington
Johanna Tydings
John Frankos
John Shorts
Joyce & Ken Mason
Jud Black
Julia Overton
Julianne & Frederick (Ricky) Haycox
Julie & Robbie Brown
Karen Feller
Karen & Lonnie Minson
Karen Vaughan
Kenneth McLeskey
Kenny Sexton
Kim Burnop
Kimberly & Scott Butler
Kimberly Grooms
Larry Davenport
Laura & Kevin Bremer
Lindsey Starkweather
Linsey & Bill Guinazzo
Lisa & Jason Gentry
Loren Hammer II
Lori Robinson
Lynn Ball
Lynn & Kevin Rowell
Lynne & Randy Dozier
Madalene & Frank Pohanka
Mary & William "Chip" Banks
Maureen & Lynn Hardaway
Meadow Cortazzo
Melissa Teets
Michael E. Shirley
Monica Karafotis
Neal Foster
Neal Klar
Neil Johnston

Neil Lessard
Newt Cagle
Nina & Tommy Ambrose
Patricia Pohanka
Paula & Barry Knight
Rachael Davanzo
Ralph Mawyer
Rhett Bailey
Richard Wright
Robert Ball
Robert Bosley
Roxanne Tyndall
Ryland Saxby
Sandy & Dennis Cipriano
Sarah Quiroga
Scotty Edwards
Shari & Darren Roney
Sherry Mills

Susan & Jimmy Slocum
Susie & James Kovacs
Suzanne & William Gooch
Sylvia Cliver
Tammy & Jr. Miller
Tanya & Rick Ray
Taylor & Drew Wilkinson
Thomas "Jimmy" Bayne
Thomas Queen
Tiffany Mosher
Valerie & Tommy Badgley
Wendy & Jim Brockenbrough
Wendy & Bill Susewind
Weston Bland
Willard Ashburn
Yvonne & Rudy Garcia

GLOSSARY

Aft: near, toward, or in the stern of a ship or the tail of an aircraft. (Merriam-Webster)
Bilge: a: the part of the underwater body of a ship between the flat of the bottom and the vertical topsides; **b:** the lowest point of a ship's inner hull. (Merriam-Webster)
Broad on the beam: at a right angle to a vessel's fore-aft axis or broad-side. (Chapman, 2006)
Bow: *nautical*: the forward part of a ship. (Merriam-Webster)
Bulkhead: a.) a transverse wall in the hull; interior compartmentalization of a vessel is created by bulkheads; in some cases, bulkheads are watertight. (Chapman, 2006)
b.) typically runs from across the inner hull to provide structural support. (JS)
Coaming: a raised edge, as around part or all of a cockpit, that prevents the seawater from entering the boat. (Chapman, 2006)
Cockpit: a.) a space for the crew, lower than the deck and often watertight or self-draining. (Chapman, 2006)
b.) an open area at the stern of a vessel with a self-draining deck close to the waterline. Typically includes a fight-chair

on sportfishing vessels. Coaming is typically thigh to waist high. (JS)

Companionway: a.) a ship's stairway from one deck to another. (Merriam-Webster)
b.) a hatch or entrance, from deck to cabin. (Chapman, 2006)
c.) a short hallway/stairs that separates the lower forward living area of the sportfishing boat from the upper salon and galley. (JS)

Console: a.) a combination of readouts or displays and an input device (such as a keyboard or switches) by which an operator can monitor and interact with a system (such as a computer or dubber). (Merriam-Webster)
b.) sportfishing boats: the main console is located on the flybridge containing the helm. (JS)

Deck: a platform in a ship serving usually as a structural element and forming the floor for its compartments. (Merriam-Webster)

Drift: (1) movement of a vessel through the water without propulsion. (2.) speed of current. (Chapman, 2006)

Fathom: a nautical linear measurement. 1 fathom = 6 feet. (Chapman, 2006)

Flying bridge/flybridge: a.) a high steering position, usually above the normal wheelhouse of a power cruiser. (Chapman, 2006)
b). sportfishing boats: typically a vessel's steering position above the main cabin/salon. (JS)

Forward: on board a vessel, the direction of the front, toward the bow. (Chapman, 2006)

Galley: the kitchen and cooking apparatus especially of a ship or airplane. (Merriam-Webster)

Gunwale: The upper edge of the side of the boat, usually a small projection above the deck; toe rail. (Chapman, 2006)

Halyard: a line used to hoist a release clip, up and away from the cockpit. (JS)

Hatch: a.) an opening in the deck of a ship or in the floor or roof of a building.
b.) the covering for such an opening. (Merriam-Webster)

Helm: a.) the area of a boat where the steering and engine controls are located; a position of control. (Merriam-Webster)

Hull: a.) the frame or body of a ship or boat exclusive of masts, yards, sails, and rigging. (Chapman, 2006)
b.) the main part of the boat that sits in the water. (JS)

Knots: unit of speed, one nautical mile per hour (1 knot = 1.151 miles per hour).
(Chapman, 2006)

Nautical mile: 6076.12 feet (1853 m), an international standard; for practical purposes, equals one minute of latitude, but not one minute of longitude. (Chapman, 2006)

Port: left, as the port side of the boat. (Chapman, 2006) (Port and left have four letters / port wine is red, the red running light if located on the left side.) (JS)

Propeller: a device that consists of a central hub with radiating blades placed and twisted so that each forms part of a helical surface and that is used to propel a vehicle (such as a ship or airplane). (Merriam-Webster) Sometimes called "wheels."

Rigging: (a.) the wire rope, rods, lines, hardware, and other equipment that support and control the spars. (Chapman, 2006)
b.) sportfishing vessel: outriggers/riggers are long poles that have a lower hinge connection at base near deck and lay out for the purpose of connecting/using a halyard. Support for the poles is provided by a series of spars, wire rope, and other rigging. (JS)

Rudder: an underwater blade that is positioned at the stern of a boat or ship and controlled by its helm and that when turned causes the vessel's head to turn in the same direction. (Merriam-Webster)

Saloon/salon: *a. chiefly British: SALON sense 1.*

c (1): a usually large public cabin on a ship (as for dining) **(2):** the living area on a yacht. A room in the cabin on a boat that's usually the primary entertaining area. "We served cocktails in the main saloon; it was a great area for entertaining our guests." (Merriam-Webster)

Sheer: the curvature of the deck, fore and aft, as seen from the side. (Chapman, 2006)

Slip: a berth for a boat between two piers or floats or piles. (Chapman, 2006)

Starboard: the right side of a vessel as related to facing the bow; the starboard side remains the starboard no matter what the orientation of a person on board. (Chapman, 2006)

Stateroom: a private room/sleeping quarters within the lower cabin area of a sportfishing boat. (JS)

Stem: the forward member of the hull, or the corresponding portion of the hull in composite construction. (Chapman, 2006)

Stern: the after portion of the boat. (Chapman, 2006) (The back of the boat.) (JS)

Transom: a.) the planking forming the stern of a square-ended boat. (Merriam-Webster)
b.) the transverse part of the stern. (Chapman, 2006)

Underway: a vessel not at anchor or aground or made fast to the shore. (Chapman, 2006)

Key:
Chapman, 2006 - *Chapman Piloting & Seamanship* 65th Edition by Elbert S. Maloney

Merriam Webster – merriam-webster.com

JS – Author (John Savage) defined

APPENDIX

LETTER TO READER
McMahon, Edward J Reverend LCDR, CHC, USN, US Dept. of the Navy, Chaplains Corps. "Invocation Prayer." Inscription on wall displayed at SEAL TEAM ONE Presidential Unit Citation Award Ceremony, JEB Little Creek, SEAL Heritage Center, NAB Coronado, California, January 9, 1975.

CHAPTER 6
Moore, John, dir. *Behind Enemy Lines*. 2001; Los Angeles, California: Davis Entertainment, 2002. DVD.

CHAPTER 17
Dictionary.com. s.v. "specific gravity (n.)" Accessed April 22, 2021. https://www.dictionary.com/browse/specific-gravity.

pinemapcap. "El Nino/La Nina and Climate Variability." March 6, 2012. Video, 50:13. https://www.youtube.com/watch?v=ykyk-o6ojI&t=148s.

US Department of the Navy. Naval Sea Systems Command. US Navy Diving Manual Revision 7, SS521-AG-PRO-010. California, December 1, 2016. https://www.navsea.navy.mil/Portals/103/Documents/SUPSALV/Diving/US%20DIVING%20MANUAL_REV7.pdf?ver=2017-01-11-102354-393.

CHAPTER 18

UK VHS Video Oddities. "BBC2 Horizon Freak Wave." Feb. 3, 2018. Video, 52:55. https://www.youtube.com/watch?v=mC8bHxgdHH4.

CHAPTER 20

Dockstrader, Jessica. "What Is the Extent of the Mental Health Crisis in Law Enforcement?" *International Public Safety Association* (blog), May 10, 2019. https://www.joinipsa.org/IPSA-Blog/7334025.

GLOSSARY

Maloney, Elbert S. *Chapman Piloting & Seamanship 65th Edition*. New York, NY: Hearst Books A Division of Sterling Publishing, 2006.

Merriam Webster. s.v. "aft (n.)" "bilge (n.)" "bow (n.)" "companionway (n.)" "console (n.)" "deck (n.)" "galley (n.)" "hatch (n.)" "helm (n.)" "propellor (n.)" "rudder (n.)" "saloon (n.)" "transom (n.)" Accessed March 4 2022. https://www.merriam-webster.com.